The United States and Chile

The United States and Chile

Imperialism and the Overthrow of the Allende Government

by James Petras
and Morris Morley

Monthly Review Press
New York and London

Library of Congress Cataloging in Publication Data
Petras, James F   1937–
 The United States and Chile.
 Includes bibliographical references.
 1. United States—Foreign relations—Chile.
2. Chile—Foreign relations—United States. 3. United
States—Foreign economic relations—Chile. 4. Chile
—Foreign economic relations—United States.   I. Morley,
Morris, joint author.   II. Title.
E183.8.C4P47   327.73′083   74-21474
ISBN 0-85345-361-6

First Printing

Monthly Review Press
62 West 14th Street, New York, N.Y. 10011
21 Theobalds Road, London WC1X 8SL

Manufactured in the United States of America

Contents

Preface

> I don't see why we need to stand by
> and watch a country go Communist
> due to the irresponsibility
> of its own people.
> —*Henry Kissinger*[1]

The role of the state in imperialist expansion has not been adequately analyzed in the growing body of literature that has emerged in the recent period. Studies focusing on the multinational corporations, their growth and behavior, have relegated the state to a peripheral position. When the state has been discussed at all, it has been viewed as a passive instrument or mere reflection of "economic interests" which in some undisclosed manner influence and direct policies. Imperial state involvement has been mentioned only at particular conjunctural "crises" moments, when it becomes apparent through dramatic action—i.e., military intervention, a coup engineered by the CIA, etc.

There has been little effort to understand the ongoing activities of the imperial state, the decision-making structure and ideology that inform specific policy decisions. Despite the far-flung and diffuse interests that the multinationals possess, and despite the enormous economic resources at their disposal, they do not possess the military, financial, ideological, and administrative apparatuses that define the imperial state. *The growth, expansion, and survival of the multinationals is in large part dependent on the action of the imperial state.* Without the military power or the administrative and ideological infrastructure developed by the imperial state, it is impossible to conceive of the multinational corporations establishing roots throughout the world. Moreover, the expansion of the multinationals requires constant injections of "aid" to subsidize accommodating national states, and develop their infrastructure.

The imperial state's elaboration and control of international financial institutions allows for the mobilization of large sums of capital; through loans it reshapes class structures as well as directs the "internal" development policies of the "recipient" countries. The products of this externally induced and directed expansion lead to sharply polarized class structures which at times threaten to "foreclose" the ongoing operations of the multinationals. The imperial state in its repressive role has acted to reverse policies, overthrow regimes—in a word, create the conditions for the continuance of multinational corporate activities. At every crucial phase in the development of multinational activity—its origin, expansion, and survival—the state has played a pivotal role. Without a committed and active state apparatus, the corporate elite would hardly have "risked" venturing out in the world of national and social upheavals subsequent to World War II. Without the international financial support, it is likely that expansion would have been much more restricted and localized. Without the imperial state organization and support of military and police apparatuses, it is highly unlikely that the multinationals could have withstood the pressures to nationalize their property. In today's world, without the imperial state the multinationals stand as impotent giants.

Our study of Chile illustrates and describes the multiplicity of operations that the imperial state engages in to sustain and nurture the multinationals. But our study also emphasizes that the state is not merely the helpmate of a series of "corporate interests," but acts largely out of a concern for the collective interests of the capitalist class, embodied in a mode of production. The analysis of the strategies and policies of the imperial state suggests that no single political agency or economic interest is decisive, but rather that imperial strategy is largely the product of an integrated body of aggregate interests of the corporate world as a whole. While U.S. corporate interests have primacy in the shaping of U.S. policy, it is the imperial state which fashions and executes that policy according to its own conceptions and time schedule. This relative "autonomy" of the imperial state accounts for the disparities between the policies proposed by ITT and the state regarding the most effective means for overthrowing Allende. While the imperial state operates in the interests of the multinational corporation, those interests are not identical; furthermore, given what we have described above, the imperial state has reserved to itself the obligation of creating or recreating the conditions for capital expansion: in that sense, state activity is frequently *prior* to and anticipates the involvement of the multinationals. This disparity between state and corporate involvement is evident in post-coup Chile. Heavy imperial state involvement is *not* matched by the multinationals: for the immediate foreseeable future, the imperial state and its financial network is the major political-economic prop for the junta. Only after a substantial and prolonged commitment by the state can we expect the insertion of private capital, despite the junta's policies of "opening" the country to unrestrained foreign exploitation.

CIA Director William Colby's revelations of U.S. subversive efforts in Chile and the contemptuous attitude of

President Ford and Kissinger toward democratic norms illustrate the fragility of bourgeois-democratic institutions when imperial structures are threatened. In secret testimony before the House Foreign Affairs Committee regarding clandestine CIA activities in Chile prior to and during the period of the Allende government, Colby admitted that the agency had initially attempted to prevent Allende from coming to power and had subsequently engaged in a continuous effort to effect his overthrow. According to Colby, CIA activities in Chile were undertaken with the express authorization of the White House *at all times*, and included: strenuous efforts to influence the outcome of the 1970 presidential election; attempts to bribe members of the Chilean Congress in order to prevent Allende's inauguration as president; penetration of all the major Chilean political parties; and continuous "destabilization" efforts, which took the form of financing anti-Allende mass media, opposition political parties, and opposition candidates in the 1973 congressional elections, and, most importantly, of supplying funds to organize and sustain every major anti-government strike, demonstration, and boycott between October 1971 and the military coup that overthrew Allende in September 1973. The Kissinger-chaired "Committee of Forty" authorized the allocation of the millions of dollars used by the CIA to carry out these activities.

Colby's revelations concerning covert U.S. activities contrast sharply with the public statements of highest-ranking policy-makers, according to whom U.S. policy was essentially one of *noninvolvement* and *nonintervention* in the internal politics of Chile up to and including the military coup:

> We deal with governments as they are. Our relations depend not on their internal structures or social systems, but on actions which affect us and the inter-American system. The new government in Chile is a clear case in point . . . we are

prepared to have the kind of relationship with the Chilean government that it is prepared to have with us.

—President Nixon
February 1971 [2]

The United States did not get involved in the so-called Alessandri formula. The United States did not seek to pressure, subvert, influence, a single member of the Chilean Congress at any time in my entire four years.

—Edward Korry
U.S. Ambassador to Chile (1967–1971)
March 1973 [3]

[The U.S. government] financed no candidates, no political parties before or after the September 8 or September 4 [elections in 1970]. . . .

Charles Meyer
Assistant Secretary of State
for Inter-American Affairs,
1969–March 1973 [4]

The CIA was heavily involved in 1964 in the election, was in a very minor way involved in the 1970 election and since then we have absolutely stayed away from any coups. Our efforts in Chile were to strengthen the democratic political parties and give them a basis for winning the election in 1976, which we expressed our hope that Allende could be defeated in a free democratic election.

—Henry Kissinger
Secretary of State-designate
September 1973 [5]

The CIA had nothing to do with the coup, to the best of my knowledge and belief. . . .

—Henry Kissinger
Secretary of State-designate
September 1973 [6]

I wish to state as flatly and as categorically as I possibly can that we did not have advance knowledge of the coup that took place on September 11 . . . either explicitly or implicitly, the U.S. government has been charged with involvement or complicity in the coup. This is absolutely false. As official spokesmen of the U.S. government have stated repeatedly, we were not involved in the coup in any way.

—Jack Kubisch
Assistant Secretary of State
for Inter-American Affairs
September 1973 [7]

. . . we are talking about the charges that have been leveled against the U.S. government around the world that were responsible for the fall of the Allende government, that we financed these activities which brought him down. I can say quite flatly that we did not . . . we had nothing to do with the political destabilization in Chile, the U.S. government had nothing to do with it.

—Harry Shlaudeman
Deputy Chief of Mission,
U.S. Embassy in Chile, 1969–1973
June 1974 [8]

Let me take the opportunity at the outset to restate that the United States government, the Central Intelligence Agency, had no role in the overthrow of the regime in Chile.

—James Schlesinger
Secretary of Defense
June 1974 [9]

. . . there's no doubt in my mind, our government had no involvement in any way whatsoever in the coup itself.

—President Ford
September 1974 [10]

In brief, an imperial policy based on subversion and deception is cloaked in democratic rhetoric to satisfy two potentially conflicting constituencies: the imperial policies are designed for the corporation, the rhetoric for the masses.

Colby's testimony on CIA involvement in Chile has further destroyed the myth perpetrated by liberals that the CIA somehow acts as an "invisible government" behind the backs of "responsible" elected and nonelected representatives. As Colby and others point out, the CIA was carrying out orders fashioned by the Committee of 40 and the White House. In the words of one U.S. official with intimate knowledge of CIA subversive activities in Allende's Chile: "The agency didn't do anything without the knowledge and consent of the 40 Committee. . . ." [11] The CIA's activities complemented the policies of other top agencies: the White House devised the economic squeeze that created dislocation and middle-class discontent and the CIA financed its mobilization and organization. The effort by *New York Times* correspondent Jonathan Kandell to minimize the CIA's role revolves around its specific functions. It is partially true, as Kandell claims, that the CIA did not "create" discontent (though *El Mercurio*, which it financed, added its bit); but it is more to the point to emphasize the CIA's efforts to organize and politically direct that discontent.

With a few exceptions, Congress played an ignoble role throughout the period during which this policy was put into practice. No serious challenges were in evidence, and when CIA activities were brought to light before a congressional oversight subcommittee, it refused to publicize or criticize the CIA role. Only because of a leak to the press did the facts come out, and no effort has been made since then to make the congressional leadership follow this up. Senator Fulbright, who has consistently refused to inquire into Kissinger's public lies and covert dealings, conceded that CIA subversion "has been going on in places other than Chile for many years" and then went on to point out that "the Senate at least has been unwilling to exercise serious control of the CIA and apparently approves of the activities to which you refer in Chile and which I believe to be a procedure which the CIA has followed in other countries." [12] No statement stands as a greater indictment of Congress's indifference to democracy and a democratic foreign policy than the above. Obviously, any effort to transform U.S. foreign policy will have to seek other political vehicles and other political parties.

President Ford has since responded to the Colby disclosures with a vigorous defense of CIA "dirty tricks" against a democratically elected government in Chile and has publicly endorsed the covert subversive action aimed at destroying the Allende government. He justified covert U.S. intervention by citing alleged Soviet/Cuban intervention, but presented no evidence to support this contention; he attacked "communism in Chile" as leading to the gradual elimination of open electoral politics in Chile, while deliberately ignoring the fact that the whole Allende period witnessed every conceivable type of election—school, trade union, and municipal and congressional elections; and he declared that U.S. intervention in Chile was in the "national interest," even though the only major U.S. interests demanding and supporting such a policy were U.S. corporate interests. Both President Ford and Secretary of State Kissinger maintain that CIA financing of opposition media interests, political parties and other groups was designed to defend democracy in Chile,[13] but these opposition elements, for whom the U.S. government evinced so much concern, were not engaged in preserving democracy but in destroying it, and the CIA reported not on stabilizing a democracy but on "destabilizing" a democracy. The Ford administration has insisted on providing aid and support to one of the bloodiest military dictatorships in Latin American history—in the name of democracy.

Active U.S. public and private involvement in Chilean internal politics before Allende was ever elected—between 1964 and 1970, in support of anti-socialist candidates and U.S. economic and political interests, and against the possibility of an Allende presidency—makes a mockery of the major U.S. government justification for intervention after 1970, the claim of defending democracy in response to specific measures taken by the Allende government. Following the electoral victory of Allende in September 1970, President Nixon's national security adviser and chief foreign policy specialist, Henry Kissinger, organized and chaired a series of weekly interagency meetings attended by high-level officials from State, Treasury, and Defense for the specific purpose of designing a policy of economic sanctions or "retaliation" against Chile. "The whole purpose of the meetings in the first couple of months after the election," according to one U.S. official, "was to insure that the various aid agencies and lending agencies were rejiggered to make sure that [Allende] wasn't to get a penny." [14] A formal National Security Council Decision Memorandum was issued prohibiting economic aid to Chile. An official close to these activities recalled Kissinger's role at that time: "Kissinger, in effect, became a Chilean desk officer . . . He made sure that policy was made in the way he and the President wanted it." [15] For a country as dependent as Chile on international financial resources to sustain short-term commercial operations and long-term development projects, the elaboration and implementation of a policy of multiple economic pressures created severe economic dislocation.

In October 1971, the U.S. government authorized an increase in CIA activity in Chile in order to complement the economic squeeze policy. According to Ray S. Cline, the highest ranking State Department intelligence official at the time, the decision to step up CIA subversive activities came from the White House: "The key role in this whole thing was in the White House . . . the orders came through Kissinger and the 40 Committee." [16] As an instrument of U.S. foreign policy, the CIA's activities in Chile were carried out under the authority and supervision of the U.S. Ambassador, Nathaniel Davis. The directive sent to Davis at this time advised him "to get a little rougher" with the Allende regime. Another U.S. official paraphrased it as saying "from now on you may aid the opposition by any means possible." [17] The CIA moved immediately to finance and mobilize those social forces adversely affected by the internal economic dislocation created by U.S. economic pressures and to direct their political energies against the Allende government.

Earlier efforts by the CIA to prevent Allende's election and subsequent inauguration gave way to a more thought-out and integrated strategy. U.S. government authorizations for CIA "destabilization" activities amounted to at least $40 million (based on the black market exchange rate) and enabled the CIA to organize the upper- and middle-class housewives' "march of the pots," to subsidize the devastating truckers' strike in late 1972 which served as a basis of massive losses in the agro-industrial area, and to subsidize a major strike by copper workers in mid-1973.[18] These actions had serious consequences for the Chilean economy and polity. The upheaval in October and November 1972 resulted in a loss in production of $300 million that negatively affected growth figures, created shortages, and promoted the military presence in the Cabinet. The 1973 lock-out resulted in $200 million damages in production, and the copper strike during the same period resulted in a loss in foreign exchange earnings of $80 million which, in turn, cut down on Chile's capacity to import and further depleted foreign reserves. All these factors combined with the external economic embargo to create societal tension and set the stage for the military coup.

The U.S. government's enthusiastic support of the military dictatorship has been accompanied by a callous disregard for its brutal and continuing repression, despite the fact that the Human Rights Commission of the Organization of American States, Amnesty International, U.S. congressional delegations, and the leaders of Chile's four largest religious congregations—among others—have documented and/or denounced the widespread torture practiced by the military, which gives every indication of being prolonged at a significant level for some time to come. In support of the junta policies, Secretary of State Kissinger angrily advised the current U.S. Ambassador to Chile, David H. Popper, "to cut out the political science lectures" after Popper had raised the issues of torture and human rights at a meeting with Chilean officials to discuss U.S. military aid to the junta.[19] Popper was only following a congressional resolution attached to the foreign aid bill, which Kissinger felt he should disregard. It is interesting to note the high esteem the junta has for its patron: Kissinger and Pinochet were named "men of the year" by the pro-junta "La Tercera de la Hora" on January 2, 1974.

Public lies, covert subversion, the destruction of democracy, and the support for a military dictatorship all have their roots in imperial capitalism's need for a regime that opens the country to exploitation. U.S. policy-makers devised a strategy designed to destroy the democratic-socialist government of Chile and return the country to its former client-state position within the U.S. sphere of influence. The major lesson to be learned by the Third World from the Chilean experience is that societies intent on revolution must follow the Cuban example—close all channels to external subversion and extend democracy only to those who abide by the process.

Methods and Data Collection

The data for this study came from a two-year search of all available documents from the following sources: U.S. Department of State, U.S. Department of the Treasury, U.S. Department of Defense, U.S. Congress (hearings, statements, etc.), World Bank, Inter-American Development Bank, *Washington Post, New York Times, Journal of Commerce, Business Week, Quarterly Economic Review of Chile* (UK), and numerous other journals, magazines, newspapers, and books. The interviews were conducted with as many of the relevant policy-makers as possible, and included interviews with officials of the U.S. Department of State, U.S. Department of the Treasury, U.S. Department of Defense, U.S. Council on International Economic Policy, U.S. Congress, World Bank, and the Inter-American Development Bank. Interviews were also conducted in Chile in the summer of 1973 with officials of the State Bank, the Ministry of Foreign Relations, and the major political parties. In all, close to seventy-five policy-makers and advisors were interviewed or consulted.

We would like to thank Nancy Hall and Pat Dolaway, who typed drafts of this manuscript amidst all their other duties.

The United States and Chile

Introduction

A number of publications have appeared which discuss the relationship between U.S. policy toward the Allende government and its subsequent overthrow by a military junta in September 1973. A substantial number of these accounts have tended to dismiss or minimize the impact of U.S. policies on Chile's internal political situation during this three year period, and to argue that the country's internal economic problems were essentially a product of the Allende government's incompetence and ineptness. This position has been repeatedly advanced by U.S. policy-makers and echoed in semiofficial publications of the government, as well as in academic circles. A sampling of this genre of argument is summarized in the following paragraphs:

> . . . the fault lies principally with an effort to redistribute income, an effort to bring about the fundamental structural changes to which the chairman referred in his opening statement. . . . the basic reasons for the deterioration of the economy lie in the policies of the Government.[1]

> . . . the economic policies themselves that were pursued by the Allende government resulted in the steadily deteriorating economic situation. The unwillingness of the government to modify its policies made it inevitable that international

lending agencies would curtail their programs for Chile. . . .
The Paris Club, consisting of various creditor nations, concluded there was little that could be done for Chile unless the
government adopted policies they could support. I repeat,
however, that it was not the United States, but the institutions themselves, which made their decisions. In sum it is
untrue to say that the U.S. Government was responsible—
either directly or indirectly—for the overthrow of Allende.[2]

. . . it was the policies of the Allende government, its
insistence on forcing the pace beyond what the traffic would
bear much more than our policies that contributed to their
economic chaos.[3]

The argument that an American invisible blockade was
responsible for or a major contributing factor to the overthrow of Allende is . . . not persuasive. . . . the economic
and political policies of the Allende government were a
failure, in and of themselves.[4]

It seems quite likely, however, that by the latter part of
1972, the credit squeeze was a drop in the bucket as far as the
causes of Chile's economic difficulties were concerned. The
real causes were the internal matters. . . . If any group can be
said to be responsible, however, it was the extreme left which
ultimately did bring down the Allende government . . . they
never gave a chance to the constitutional road to socialism.
. . . In sum: the total credit picture of Chile may not have
been anything like as bad as is sometimes made out: certainly
not by the latter part of 1972. The real problem was lagging
exports due to copper production losses; and soaring imports
of food because of the failure of agriculture and Dr. Allende's
desire to *more* than compensate for this—despite the lack of
means.[5]

Economically, Allende was pressing a policy that was bound
to drive it over a cliff.[6]

Salvador Allende died not because he was a socialist, but because he was an incompetent. . . . the program of the Allende Government was not well worked out. . . . By August 1973, Mr. Allende's power was gone. . . . The people almost wished for a military coup.[7]

Essentially, these accounts, by commission and omission, in effect absolve the U.S. government and private enterprise of having had any significant impact on the course of events in Chile. By arguing that it was the Allende government which created the conditions for the military coup, the implication is that the coup was "inevitable" and (among some writers) justified. In more general terms the arguments imply that efforts to redistribute income and promote rapid and effective changes such as those envisioned by the democratic socialist government are doomed to failure because of their intrinsic impracticality.

It is not our purpose here to consider the totally inadequate discussion in the above-mentioned accounts of the economic and political behavior of the internal opposition (political formations, social classes, and military officials), and their impact on the economy. What we are interested in documenting is the fact that Chile was heavily in debt *prior* to Allende's coming to power; that these debts did not significantly stimulate economic development; that most of these debts were contracted with public, private, and international banks subject to U.S. influence; that payments on these unproductive debts incurred by earlier regimes came due during the Allende period; that the U.S. demand for debt payments became one instrument of U.S. economic pressure; that the cut-off of credits and loans was part of an overall U.S. policy to undermine the Allende government; that U.S. policy was neither haphazard nor improvised but followed directly from the highest policy-making circles which incorporated the *political-economic interests of the*

United States in the region as a whole as their primary consideration; that U.S. officials *chose* to reject the Chilean experience, promote the Brazilian, and negotiate the Peruvian for essentially political as well as economic reasons; that changes in U.S. policy to Chile subsequent to the coup reflected the change in the political and economic orientation of the regime; that U.S. military programs and personnel complemented the activities of political and economic officials and contributed toward the same policy goal; and that U.S. policy contributed substantially and directly to the overthrow of the Allende government.

The major thrust of this study is highly critical of the accounts minimizing the role of the United States. The socialist government of Chile represented the focal point of the new nationalist challenge to the United States in Latin America. Chile's tentative efforts to move out of the capitalist orbit and its support of ideological pluralism weakened the ties between the Northern and Southern Hemispheres. It directly challenged U.S. political hegemony and the ability of U.S. policy-makers to secure the continent economically for U.S. interests. Democratic socialism represented a systemic challenge, a conflict between two different modes of production.[8] U.S. policy-makers refused to countenance nationalization of U.S. economic assets in a country where *nationalization was linked to a socialist, anticapitalist development strategy.* The overall U.S. response to the Allende government in Chile was twofold: a combination of severe economic pressures whose cumulative impact would result in internal economic chaos and a policy of disaggregating the Chilean state through creating ties with specific critical sectors (the military), and supporting their efforts at weakening the capacity of the state to realize a nationalist development project. This sustained policy of direct and indirect intervention culminated in a general societal crisis, a coup, and a military government.

Entering the 1970s, the United States was faced with a new nationalist challenge in Latin America. Nationalist or regionalist fronts emerging at the end of the 1960s could be divided into three distinct but interrelated groups: nationalist regimes (Bolivia, Peru, and Chile); burgeoning nationalist movements (Uruguay and Argentina); and follower nations (Ecuador, Colombia, Venezuela, and Panama). Within the group of "leader" nationalist countries Chile, with its combined political and economic challenge to the United States based on mass popular participation, emerged as the core nation. To a lesser extent, the Bolivian government of General Torres represented a potential similar challenge. The Peruvian military junta, on the other hand, combined a policy of marginating large sectors of the population from effective participation in the political arena with an economic strategy designed to control and limit the access of foreign capital within a mixed economy. Nationalizations of foreign properties were interspersed with new concessions to foreign capital as the junta began to move, politically, to the right.

In Uruguay, a military-controlled civilian government moved decisively to weaken the electoral threat represented by the Frente Amplio and nationalist sectors of the political opposition. In Argentina, the anti-Marxism of Perón and the lack of significant foreign investment controls have been accompanied by a policy designed to crush the power of the nationalist Left. The U.S. strategy of eliminating the nationalist threat in Chile, Bolivia, and Uruguay, and increasing the pressures on Peru and Argentina has proved extremely successful. In order of vulnerability, the challenges in Bolivia and Uruguay were eliminated prior to the overthrow of the Allende government. In order of importance, however, Chile had priority status.

To understand the role played by the United States in the overthrow of the government of President Allende, it is important to consider the way in which the Chilean economy was dependent on the United States and its political system open to U.S. influence. Chilean society, perhaps more than any other in Latin America (on a per capita basis), was vegetating on borrowed time or, more specifically, borrowed money. The standard of living of the heavily consumer-oriented upper and middle classes was not based on an expanding productive system but on foreign loans, credits, and delayed payments. Throughout the sixties the foreign debt soared and new loans chased after old debts in a spiraling sequence that left little investment for industrial expansion or agricultural growth. A historical analysis of Chile's increasing financial dependence during the decade preceding the Allende government is essential for measuring the impact of U.S. policies adopted after 1970. The dimensions of the problem of dependence include in general form:

1. The absolute size of the external debt, the payments schedule, and the sources of refinancing;
2. the impact of the previous decades' loans in developing the productive capacity of the country to determine whether it generated new sources of capital for repayments;
3. the sources of short-term credits and their impact on consumption and production; and
4. the impact of previous trade patterns on the problems of replacement parts in strategic industrial-mineral-transport sectors.

Chilean economic dependence on the United States remained a significant factor during the period of the Allende government. U.S. direct private investment in Chile in 1970 stood at $1.1 billion, out of a total estimated foreign investment of $1.672 billion.[9] Despite the diversification of investment in the 1960s, away from extractive industries and related service industries and toward manufacturing, trade, and banking, the bulk of U.S. private investment in Chile remained in the mining and smelting sector (over 50 percent). The balance was directed primarily into consumer-type activities and manufacturing.[10] However, U.S. and foreign corporations controlled almost all of the most dynamic and critical areas of the economy by the end of 1970: machinery and equipment (50 percent); iron, steel, and metal products (60 percent); petroleum products and distribution (over 50 percent); industrial and other chemicals (60 percent); rubber products (45 percent); automotive assembly (100 percent); radio and television (nearly 100 percent); pharmaceuticals (nearly 100 percent); office equipment (nearly 100 percent); copper fabricating (100 percent); tobacco (100 percent); and advertising (90 percent).[11] Furthermore, U.S. corporations controlled 80 percent of the production of Chile's only important foreign exchange earner: copper. Hence, the Allende government was confronted with a situation of external control over copper production, technology and spare parts, and manufacturing, making the economy extremely vulnerable to financial and commercial pressures.

Although the level of Chile's imports from the United States declined from approximately 40 percent of total imports during the Frei period to approximately 13 percent in 1972, this quantitative decline in trade with the United States is deceptive because Chile continued to depend on the importation of essential replacement parts from North American firms. In addition, the precipitous decline in short-term U.S. commercial credits (from 78.4 percent of the total in 1970 to approximately 6.6 percent in 1972) seriously affected the Allende government's ability to purchase replacement parts and machinery for the most critical sectors of the economy: copper, steel, electricity, petroleum, and transportation. By late 1972, for example, it was estimated that almost one-third of the diesel trucks at Chuquicamata copper mine, 30 percent of privately owned microbuses, 21 percent of all taxi buses, and 33 percent of state-owned buses in Chile (where the majority of buses and trucks originate from U.S. General Motors or U.S. Ford models), were unable to operate because of the lack of spare parts or tires. Over 90 percent of spare parts in the copper industry were imported from the United States. In overall terms, the value of U.S. machinery and transport equipment exported to Chile by U.S. firms declined from $152.6 million in 1970 to $110.0 million in 1971.[12]

Chile, probably more than most underdeveloped countries, was dependent on external financial sources to maintain month to month commercial operations as well as to finance so-called long-term development projects.

The export sector of the Chilean economy (mostly copper) was controlled, in part, by U.S. corporations; thus the main source of foreign exchange earnings was also controlled by U.S. firms. Production planning, marketing, and sales were also under U.S. corporate control. About 95 percent of the replacement parts for machinery in the copper industry were imported from the United States. Given the high degree of integration that existed between the Chilean export sector and the U.S. economy, and given the Chilean economy's inordinate dependence on the export of copper for foreign exchange earnings to import crucial foodstuff, raw materials, parts, etc., externally induced abrupt and severe shocks or dislocations in the mining sector would have significant ramifications throughout the economy. The externally linked enclave in effect was a "hostage" of the metropolitan countries: its high-level technology and "reach" into foreign markets made it highly vulnerable to actions and reactions in the metropolitan countries. The crucial theoretical point is that when countries evolve a pattern of development largely induced by external sources of finance, technology, and machinery, and when they fail to develop out of the accumulated debts the productive capacity to satisfy debt obligations and new investment needs, a condition of vulnerability is engendered which makes the economy relatively easy to disrupt and highly susceptible to crisis. The points of foreign contact or entry, the transactions and exchanges that take place, become during the ensuing conflict points of access through which external groups can adversely affect the internal performance of the economy.

The first section of this study is a discussion of debt accumulation in the period prior to the election of Salvador Allende. This discussion serves to highlight the nondevelopmental or political basis of loans and grants. In other words, the external debt not only becomes a political weapon once consummated, but from its very inception, during the process of debt accumulation, political ties between the United States and Chilean sociopolitical forces were primary considerations. The debt basis of U.S.-Chilean relationships became the cause and consequence of the "porous" nature of Chilean economic, social, and military institutions. The grants and loans resulted from commonly decided programs based on intense interaction and mutual consultation between Chilean and U.S. officials. The externally linked channels of communication (as much as the networks themselves), devised to facilitate the transfer of funds, became the points of access to Chilean decision-making and decision-makers.

The sudden and abrupt termination of external funds seriously disrupted the institutionally accepted mode of operation, leaving a huge gap in the day to day operations of the economic system.

The combined impact of internal and external pressures began to seriously affect Chilean production after mid-1972 and increasingly thereafter.

The downward trend in industrial production, as Table 1 makes abundantly clear, begins with the mobilization of the

Table 1
Industrial Production in 1972 [13]
(percent change on 1971)

January	21.7
February	15.9
March	13.0
April	17.1
May	14.4
June	5.3
July	5.3
August	3.6
September	−8.7
October	−7.8
November	−8.1
December	−11.1

opposition and reaches a high point during the period of the intensification of opposition activity (September–December), designed to undermine the government's position.

Chile can be compared to a drug addict: daily injections of new foreign loans were necessary to nourish the "habit" cultivated by previous regimes. The economy had lost the capacity to sustain itself by its own efforts. The "rehabilitation" of the Chilean economy, given the extreme form of financial dependence on which it was founded, would have needed a painful shift of priorities that would have required at least a decade, time and circumstances which were not available to the Allende government. Short of a complete rupture in relations, a government which attempts to reconstruct society, and meet past financial obligations without continuing sources of funding, as well as operate through the established channels and networks, will ultimately suffer dire economic and political consequences: the economic constraints will create severe internal bottlenecks and the political channels will serve to undermine the regime.

The second section of this study deals with the decision-making structure that formulates U.S. policy. Contrary to the assertion of some commentators, the proliferation of policy statements and action proposals is not evidence of bureaucratic anarchy or the lack of any fixed policy-making center. When the stakes at hand appeared to involve major challenges to the fundamental tenets of U.S. political economy (as was perceived to be the case in Chile), a centralized policy command was established, a "general line" was elaborated, and a variety of policy-making agencies were delegated to implement a variety of complementary tasks derived from the general policy. The National Security Council formulated general policy which was transmitted to several governmental agencies (Treasury, CIA, State, Defense), which in turn elaborated concrete measures which were then put into practice in the field, through Treasury appointees in the international banks, CIA operatives infiltrating Chilean parties, or military advisors attached to the Chilean military command. The multiple dimensions of dependency and the porous nature of Chilean political, economic, and social institutions facilitated successful implementation of many of the negative measures which the U.S. agencies formulated.

Private sector activity served to pressure government action and in turn responded to government policy measures. The initiative taken by affected enterprises crystalized action by high policy-makers: once it became government policy to isolate the Allende government, the private sector as a whole (commercial banks, firms, etc.) was mobilized and fell into line. The state was instrumental in converting the action of a fraction of the ruling class into the position of the class as a whole.

The specific U.S. policy responses to the Chilean effort at socialist transformation took several interrelated forms:

1. Diplomatic and political pressure aimed at maximizing international isolation of Chile;
2. economic squeeze to provoke economic dislocation and social conflict;

3. military aid to disaggregate the Chilean state, strengthen bonds between U.S. and Chilean military, and lay the basis for a coup; and
4. maintenance of political and diplomatic relations to collect information, maintain ties with political opposition, and facilitate the flow of financial resources to allies.

The negotiating posture simulated by U.S. officials in their dealings with their Chilean counterparts served to encourage the illusory hope among the Chileans that a long-term settlement was possible which would lead to a reopening of lines of credit, loans, etc. In light of the evidence, which suggests that no such settlement was envisioned by U.S. policy-makers, we can conclude that the negotiations merely served as an information-gathering service: a means of measuring the relative strength of the regime, its capacity to resist pressure, and its willingness to abandon positions, as well as to identify divisions within the government and to exploit them.

U.S. policy was not determined by any particular economic decision in Chile, Latin America, or the United States. The overall policy of aggressive economic intervention articulated by the National Security Council and put into practice by U.S. agencies was derived from a commitment to oppose structural ideological developments in Chile: the transformation of Chile into a democratic socialist society. The changes envisioned by the Allende government not only restricted the capacity of U.S. capital to expand in Chile but threatened to disarticulate the economic and trade patterns within the region. Changes in Chile potentially laid the basis for modifying and redefining Latin America's external economic relations. Under Allende Chile was still in transition, both in and out of the U.S. orbit, and this accounts for its vulnerability to U.S. pressures.

U.S. policy to socialist countries or societies in transition to socialism varies according to the porosity of the state, the possibilities of reversing institutional changes, and the timing or consummation of transformation. Accordingly we can classify three different types of imperial strategies with three different types of socialist societies:

1. Permeable State (Chile): A state in which changes are reversible, sectors of state apparatus are linked to old class structure, and, externally, political channels are open (parties, pressure groups, press, etc.).

Imperial Strategy: Maintain relations, disaggregate the state, avoid precipitous action that would lead to a premature rupture in relations, coalesce internal forces, contest external sources of funding. In the short run the notion is to maintain relations as a conduit for nourishing internal sources feeding into the disarticulated state and to avoid adverse polarization (nation vs. U.S.). The middle-range strategy is to prepare for a "historic confrontation," mobilizing social forces willing to reverse the institutional changes which have been brought into being, to dismantle and totally disaggregate the state. The strategic goal is to reconstitute the state in the image and the service of imperial foreign economic and diplomatic interests.

2. Nonpermeable State ("Recent"—Cuba): In the imperial lexicon, a "totalitarian" state. A state in which irreversible changes have occurred, there is no possibility of disaggregating the state (for example, a popular militia has replaced the previous standing army), and political channels are closed (parties and opposition pressure groups are disarticulated).

Imperial Strategy: Rupture relations, mount international campaign to isolate target country, develop propaganda war focusing on closed nature of society (which amounts to protest over loss of points of entry).

3. Nonpermeable State (Long-term—Soviet Union): Internal characteristics are similar to type two: nonreversible changes, durable institutions, no points of access, etc.

Imperial Strategy: Possible accommodation (coexistence), reopen relations on basis of recognition of imperial spheres of influence, attempt long-term penetration of markets and obtain access to raw materials through loans and technological sales, short-term propaganda wars continue to explore internal differentiation.

Considering the situation of both the country in transition to socialism and the imperial country attempting to maintain its network, the possible choices open are quite limited. For the former the problem becomes one of rupturing relations at the historic moment when a maximum of internal forces can be polarized against the external enemy and their principal internal allies. The efforts by the Chilean government to substitute tactical gains through negotiations were based on the mistaken and premature assumption of the possibility of coexistence between a permeable state and an imperial country. For the latter, the maintenance of relations with Allende's Chile was an opportunity to reverse an increasingly socialized economy. By taking advantage of the multiple points of opposition permitted by the government, the United States channeled funds selectively to specific institutions (army, Catholic university) which would serve as spearheads or points of support for the counterrevolution. Recipient institutions of external funding were sufficiently homogeneous in political composition to assure the donors that the funds would only strengthen the opposition. Covert subsidies promoted the mass activity tolerated by the government; these subsidies contributed in rapid succession to politicizing, activating, and mobilizing substantial social forces leading to the creation of organizational focos which in turn captured the leadership of voluntary associations and disciplined the membership through a process of selective rewards and punishments. The subsidized and organized forces then focused their activities on the nerve centers of the economic infrastructure, transport and distribution. The armed forces entered the government to protect the social mobilization of the opposition and increase the porosity of the government. The military's penetration of government opened further channels for covert subsidies and subsequent activities become more audacious, causing government authority to crumble. The government was paralyzed from within by subversive members of the state apparatus and undermined from the outside by the attacks on the nerves of the economy.

Imperial policy is premised on the short-run need to disaggregate the state, disassemble critical institutions of the state apparatus, and create commitments and loyalties to the interests of the external power. These sociopolitical bonds facilitate the channeling back into the country, through the disarticulated state apparatus, the policies which will best serve them. This "alienated" apparatus (serving external needs) subsequently dismantled or reshaped the institutions of the Allende government to serve their central political project: the reconstruction of a state apparatus as an instrument of private economic accumulation and expansion through mass repression. The whole of the state apparatus was remade in the image of the alienated fragment. Hence the new state can only be an alien state: the reconstructed state apparatus assumes the orientation of the disaggregated segment bound to the external power. From disaggregating the nation-state, the imperial country contributes to reconstructing and strengthening the state apparatus: homogeneous, centralized bodies linked at the top and extended outward to the metropolis emerge. In the language of imperial social science, the country has now reached the period of "institution building."

Overall foreign economic relations are not only conditioned by political considerations, they frequently influence and shape them. In the context of considering the evolving U.S. foreign economic policies toward Chile, the crucial consideration for U.S. policy-makers was the elaboration of economic measures to consolidate or change (depending on the government), the class basis of state power and only secondarily to promote economic development or specific U.S. economic interests. The U.S. credit and trade squeeze was designed for a political purpose (not designed to serve specific economic interests): to promote the political demise of a democratic socialist government. Economic pressures led to economic dislocation (scarcities), which generated the social basis (discontent among the lower middle class), that created the political context for a military coup. In a porous dependent society U.S. economic policy was a formidable instrument in shifting the internal balance of power against the change-oriented government. The inequalities in economic and military power between imperial and dependent countries once transferred into the sphere of internal struggles will tend to turn the balance against the anti-imperial forces. The Chilean experience suggests that only in the process of rupturing external relations and the concomitant closure of internal access points could the transition to socialism continue.

The separation of external pressure from internal social struggles is inadequate for understanding the events in Chile or any other dependent country. Imperial-induced shortages that adversely affected specific types of economic activities and/or social classes provoking social unrest and leading to political confrontations are indistinguishable from similar shortages caused by domestic wholesalers, distributors, etc. The external forces were very much involved, even if their presence was not always physically visible. The yet unknown extent to which active agents of the United States penetrated political and social organizations is secondary to the fact that such activity complemented the larger economic pressures generated by activists based in the United States.

1
The U.S. Role in Chile, 1964–1970

There were several important events and experiences in Chilean political history during the six years prior to Allende's election which are critical to understanding the subsequent development of U.S.-Chilean relations: the role of the United States in the presidential elections of 1964; the extent and purpose of U.S. "development" financing in Chile; and the impact of these efforts on Chilean development. The main conclusion is that U.S. political-economic involvement in Chile was successful in influencing short-run political events (electing Frei in 1964), but was a failure in its subsequent efforts to promote socioeconomic development, thus setting the stage for a major political defeat, the election of Allende in 1970. The costs of U.S. economic involvement in Chilean politics, in the form of a huge foreign debt, were shifted to the shoulders of the Chilean people after Allende was elected. Hence we have the paradoxical result of the United States paying and winning, and then losing and collecting: external financing of development had more than one hidden advantage for the donor country.

Toward the end of the conservative Alessandri presidency (1958–1964), the U.S. government and U.S. corporations with large economic investments in Chile became increas-

ingly concerned over a possible move to the Left in the 1964
national elections. These fears were reinforced by the
outcome of a special congressional election in the tradition-
ally conservative rural province of Curicó in March 1964,
where the vote for the Left coalition (FRAP) candidate rose
by over 10 percent as compared to the 1963 results, while the
Radical-Liberal-Conservative candidate's share of the vote
declined by 17 percent.[1] U.S. policy-makers were initially
divided over whether to support the presidential candidate of
the right-wing Democratic Front, Julio Duran, or the leader
of the Christian Democratic Party, Eduardo Frei. The CIA,
high-level echelons of the State Department, and the U.S.
Ambassador to Chile, Charles Cole, favored Duran, while
most other influential policy-makers within the Kennedy
administration were oriented toward Frei. However, the
Curicó debacle had significant consequences for the upcoming presidential election. The Democratic Front disbanded,
Duran withdrew his candidacy, and the Chilean Right moved
to support Frei. Within the U.S. government, a similar
coalescence of support behind the candidacy of Eduardo
Frei occurred. Frei's major opponent in the 1964 presidential
election was the candidate of the FRAP coalition, Salvador
Allende.

U.S. government and corporate intervention on behalf of
Frei in the 1964 election took a number of forms. Approximately $20 million in U.S. funds was channeled into the Frei
campaign, while at least 100 U.S. "special personnel" were
posted to Chile from Washington and other Latin American
countries to engage in complementary activities.[2] "U.S.
government intervention in Chile in 1964 was blatant and
almost obscene," a key U.S. intelligence officer at the time
recalled. "We were shipping people off right and left, mainly
State Department but also CIA with all sorts of covers."[3]
CIA operations took the form of subsidizing, via conduits
such as the International Development Foundation, peasant

organizations, or financing pro-Frei media operations. Philip B. F. Agee, a former CIA intelligence officer with responsibility for Latin America, has stated that he personally acted as a conduit for the channeling of $200,000 in Chilean currency from a major New York City bank into covert electoral activities in support of Frei. "Agee handled the cashing of the check in Montevideo, where he was then assigned to the CIA station, and conversion into Chilean currency which was then sent on by diplomatic pouch into Santiago, he related." [4] The State Department role was no less pervasive. An important policy-maker on Latin America at the time of the Chilean election distinguished between its public position and its contribution to an interventionist policy:

> The State Department maintained a facade of neutrality and proclaimed it from time to time. . . . Individual officers —and economic counselors—would look for opportunities. And where it was a question of passing money, forming a newspaper or community development program, the operational people would do the work. AID [Agency for International Development] found itself suddenly overstaffed, looking around for peasant groups or projects for slum dwellers. . . . Once you established a policy of building support among peasant groups, government workers and trade unions, the strategies fell into place.[5]

Executives of the U.S. copper companies in Chile also played an active role in the pre-election period. Indirectly, they bolstered Frei's position by accepting his program of "Chileanization" of the copper industry as the only viable alternative to nationalization. Moreover, "Privately, top Washington officials admit Frei's election was greatly helped by the 'serious efforts' of U.S. copper interests and the U.S. Information Agency." [6]

An unusual influx of U.S. military personnel into Chile was also a characteristic of the period prior to the election. During 1963, an extra forty-five U.S. military officers (over and above the sixteen military attachés assigned to the U.S. embassy), were posted to Chile and sent to various U.S. military missions around the country. A further delegation of thirty-five U.S. armed services officers arrived in the country approximately two to three months before the election. Coincidently, at the time of the election, the Chilean armed forces were engaged in "antisubversion exercises" and joint army-navy exercises were projected during the period when the Chilean congress would be forced to vote for a new president if no candidate received an absolute majority of the total electoral vote.[7]

Between 1961 and 1970, Chile was the largest recipient of any country in Latin America, on a per capita basis, of U.S. Alliance for Progress loans, approximately $1.3 to $1.4 billion.[8] During the early years of the Alliance, the U.S. Agency for International Development (AID) justified substantial economic assistance to Chile on the basis of the country's ten year development plan, even though the plan "did not set forth clear priorities or definite projects. . . ." AID efforts to reorganize those sectors of the Chilean bureaucracy involved in the development process were "ineffectual," and by the mid-1960s the attempt had "virtually collapsed." The structural problems of the Chilean government agencies were paralleled by the incapacity of AID to develop its own strategies for rational economic development. AID evaluations of various Chilean government programs and specific projects were "inadequate" and "provided little foundation for decisions in the way of objective research and analysis."[9] Nevertheless, AID funds to Chile continued to increase, from $41.3 million in 1963 to $78.8 million in 1964.[10]

By 1963, U.S. policy-makers decided to change their strategy from making development assistance dependent upon structural administrative changes in the Chilean bu-

AID

reaucracy, to one of making it dependent "upon Chile's accomplishing several narrowly defined fiscal and monetary goals aimed at stabilizing domestic prices and effecting exchange reform." [11] The aid disbursements for 1963, 1964, and 1965 were all essentially based on Chilean acceptance of fiscal and monetary stabilization policies rooted in the adherence to yearly IMF "standby" agreements. Yet the result was neither stabilization nor development. The annual rate of inflation during 1963 and 1964 was 40 percent (an increase over the two previous years), the trade deficit increased, and the economic growth rate declined. A congressional study was severely critical of the U.S. government decision to attach the same conditions for the 1963 and 1964 AID disbursements, given the performance of the Chilean economy in 1963 as well as the unlikely event of structural economic reforms being implemented during an election year. The study concluded that the major rationale behind the program was political: to bolster the position of the nonleftist forces in the 1964 presidential election.

Clearly, the 1964 assistance package ($55 million program loan; $15 million Export-Import Bank line of credit; $15 million Treasury exchange agreement) must have been based solely on political considerations—to maintain Chile's current levels of economic activity and investment and to support the balance of payments so that financial deterioration and unemployment would not occur in an election year. [12]

Total assistance to Chile from the U.S. government was actually far in excess of the above figures. In this respect, it is interesting to note the expenditure levels over the three year period 1963 to 1965. Overall aid increased dramatically from $97.7 million in 1963 to $260.4 million in 1964, and then decreased just as rapidly to $92.5 million in 1965. [13] The 1964 allocation included a $40 million general economic development grant to alleviate the unemployment situation. "We

did not want to have a condition of vast unemployment as
Chile was going into the election," recalled a former AID
official.[14] Another example of the political nature of the aid
allocation in 1964 was a $15 million loan in May for
commodity imports because of a U.S. "desire to dampen the
inflation in the pre-election period by financing additional
imports. . . ." [15]

AID continued to push for increased and disproportionate
economic assistance to Chile throughout the 1960s. As a
predecessor to the Overseas Private Investment Corporation
(OPIC), AID also issued $1.8 billion in political risk insur-
ance in Chile during the 1965–1970 period. A study prepared
for the House Foreign Affairs Committee concluded that
this insurance was "part of U.S. policy to help support the
government of Eduardo Frei's Christian Democratic Party,
although no ratified bilateral agreement existed between the
two governments." [16] One AID official involved in this
activity recounted that in the last three months of 1967
"everyone was pushing us to issue as much insurance in Chile
as we could." [17]

The AID presentation to Congress for increased financial
appropriations for Chile in fiscal 1971, made just prior to the
1970 election, was accompanied by a recognition on the
agency's part "that the Alliance had failed dismally in its
objectives in this country. . . ." [18] The inflation rate in 1969
was the highest since Frei took office; government policies in
the agricultural sector (land reform, per capita production,
etc.) had failed visibly; and the growth rate of the Gross
National Product for the period 1965–1969 compared unfavorably to the period 1961–1965.[19]

The Frei government was also the recipient of substantial
amounts of development assistance in the form of loans and
grants from U.S. government banks and U.S.-influenced
international financial institutions. The U.S. Export-Import

Bank made loans totaling $254.4 million to Chile between 1967 and 1969. The World Bank and the Inter-American Development Bank were also active. Between 1965 and 1970, the loans to Chile by each institution amounted to $98 million and $192.1 million, respectively.[20] By December 1970 Chile had accumulated a public and private debt of $3.83 billion, most of it owed to U.S. government agencies and private lenders.[21]

As the evidence of congressional hearings and testimony, interviews, and news accounts indicates, U.S. economic policy was politically motivated: directed at promoting an antisocialist candidate, government, and policies and preventing a socialist from succeeding. The heavy direct and indirect financial subsidies of the Frei candidacy and later presidency against Allende and the Left by the U.S. government and corporations, and the joint military activities were early indications of the policies that the United States would adopt during the Allende presidency. Only then the process was reversed: loans to the government were cut off, aid was channeled to the military, and covert funding was directed to opposition groups. The combined efforts of private and public officials in favor of Frei and against Allende in 1964 continued (with some modifications) with the election of Allende. The continuity of U.S. policy, and its opposition to the Left before Allende came to power, makes untenable the argument that Allende's specific policy measures were responsible for U.S. policy. Both during the 1960s and 1970s there is a consistent pattern in U.S. policy of active involvement in support of U.S. economic and political interests, utilizing loans, credits, subsidies, and military programs. U.S. economic involvement contributed to the election of Eduardo Frei in 1964 (though it was insufficient to prevent Allende's victory in 1970), and to the downfall of Allende in September 1973. The United States is an active partisan participant in the major internal political struggles in Chile, utilizing its economic resources in an effort to buttress its political and class allies through electoral contests when possible and through military means when necessary.

2

U.S. Policy and the Election of Allende, September – November 1970

Having failed in their efforts to influence the elections through financial subsidies to the nonsocialist candidates, U.S. policy-makers and CIA and private corporate officials were thrown into disarray with the victory of Allende. Kissinger and his foreign policy advisors were forced to improvise policy within very limited time constraints and with few immediate prospects. The initial response was one of defining the political situation resulting from the election. Kissinger's definition of political reality included three elements: (1) maximum priority was assigned to Chilean political developments; (2) Chile was specified as a maximum danger area within the region; and (3) political developments in the region were linked to the evolution of events in Chile.

Hence for U.S. policy-makers the political situation in Chile was of strategic importance to the possible relations which would develop between the United States and Latin America.

The confusion which reigned among U.S. private and public officials resulted in the absence, initially, of a coordinated and combined effort. The State Department sought to influence Christian Democrats and parliamentarians to vote against the confirmation of Allende. The ambassador, while supporting those efforts, also maintained contact with ITT and took other initiatives. ITT proposed more aggressive direct intervention by the U.S. government, offered subsidies to the CIA, pressured the ambassador, and favored efforts directed toward an immediate overthrow. The CIA established contacts with the banking and corporate world hoping to precipitate an economic crisis which would force the Christian Democrats to deny Allende the presidency. This multiprong economic strategy did not prevent the CIA from developing contacts with the Chilean military which, however, was not politically and organizationally prepared for a coup. The precipitous efforts of ITT, predicated on the possibility of an immediate coup, came into conflict with the efforts of the CIA, which apparently favored a policy of creating more propitious political conditions for a military coup. The element of miscalculation and surprise and the improvisation of policy measures failed to prevent Allende from taking office.

The U.S. government and various U.S. corporations with extensive economic interests in Chile expressed considerable interest in influencing the outcome of the Chilean presidential election prior to September. In anticipation of a possible victory by Salvador Allende and the Unidad Popular, a series of meetings took place in May and June 1970 between ITT Director and former head of the CIA, John A. McCone, and the then CIA Director, Richard Helms. Their discussions centered around the question of how the U.S. government could actively support the candidacy of either of Allende's opponents, Conservative Jorge Alessandri or Christian Democrat Radomiro Tomic. On June 4, this topic was discussed at a specially convened meeting of the U.S. government's interdepartmental "Committee of Forty" which is responsible for approving covert CIA global operations. The meeting was chaired by the president's national security advisor, Henry Kissinger.[1] Although a full account of the proceedings is not yet available, the committee authorized a CIA plan to use $400,000 in support of anti-Allende media activities during the election campaign. It is conceivable that other activities were ruled out until after the election because the U.S. embassy in Chile, on the basis of a series of polls carried out by the CIA, was predicting an Alessandri plurality of approximately 40 percent of the popular vote.[2]

The initial U.S. government response to Allende's success was one of shock and hostility. The Nixon administration immediately began to make efforts to block his confirmation by voicing fears that Allende's presidency would eventually culminate in a communist government in Chile, and raising the specter of similar developments occurring in Argentina, Peru, and Bolivia. The Committee of Forty held an urgent meeting to discuss the implications of the Chilean results for U.S. policy and to plan countermoves. In Chile, U.S. Ambassador Edward Korry drafted a memorandum to the State Department containing a negative assessment of the Allende victory and its long-term consequence: "I said that over the course of six years there would be an irreversible political structure [in Chile]. . . ."[3]

Henry Kissinger, the president's national security advisor, played a key role in formulating the general contours of U.S. policy toward a socialist Chile. In a White House briefing on September 16, he described Allende as "probably a Communist" who represented "a non-democratic party, which tends to make his election pretty irreversible." Kissinger suggested that an Allende presidency would signal the end of open electoral politics in Chile and argued that a communist Chile would have a direct impact on the future direction of Argentina ("which is already deeply divided"), Peru ("which has already been heading in directions that have been difficult to deal with"), and Bolivia ("which has also gone in a more leftist, anti-U.S. direction"). The problem was global and hemispheric, but the transformation of policy goals into concrete policy actions would require a more favorable conjuncture of events than existed.

> . . . I don't think we should delude ourselves that an Allende takeover in Chile would not present massive problems for us, and for democratic forces and for pro-U.S. forces in Latin America, and indeed to the whole Western Hemisphere. What would happen to the Western Hemisphere Defense Board, or to the Organization of American States, and so forth, is extremely problematical. So we are taking a close look at the situation. It is not one in which our capacity for influence is very great at this particular moment now that matters have reached this particular point.[4]

A congressional study was led to observe that "it is, accordingly, clear that both the U.S. embassy in Santiago and high levels of the U.S. government in Washington viewed with hostility the prospects of an Allende government." [5] This hostility was the basis of U.S. policy efforts to overthrow the Allende government.

The U.S. business community responded similarly, speaking of "the serious implications of Allende's ascension to power for the United States and United States business." [6] One multinational corporation with substantial economic assets in Chile, International Telephone and Telegraph, decided on a concerted policy aimed at preventing Allende's inauguration as president. With the active support of the U.S. government, they hoped to reinstate a government supportive of the status quo and U.S. investor interests in Chile. Beginning in mid-1970, ITT officials proceeded to establish contacts within the National Security Council, the State Department ("We maintained daily and almost hourly communication with State as regards Chile," wrote ITT Senior Vice-President Edward Gerrity), the United States Information Agency, the Overseas Private Investment Corporation, the Central Intelligence Agency, the Inter-American Development Bank, the Senate Foreign Relations Committee, and the House Foreign Affairs Committee. Furthermore, their relationships with U.S. embassy personnel in Chile were close and long-standing: "During Ambassador Korry's visits to Washington we always conferred with him. We have close relationships with various officers of the Santiago Embassy and we have conferred with them both in Washington and in Santiago." [7]

Immediately after the September election, an ITT official contacted Kissinger's senior advisor on Latin America, Viron Vaky, to inform him that ITT was prepared to financially support any U.S. government plan to prevent Allende's inauguration as president by the Chilean congress.

> I told Mr. Vaky to tell Mr. Kissinger Mr. Geneen [ITT Chairman] is willing to come to Washington to discuss ITT's interest and that we are prepared to assist financially in sums up to seven figures. I said Mr. Geneen's concern is not one of "after the barn door has been locked," but that all along we have feared the Allende victory and have been trying unsuccessfully to get other American companies aroused over the fate of their investments and join us in pre-election efforts.[8]

Meanwhile, U.S. Ambassador Korry (according to an ITT memorandum), was actively engaged in the effort to thwart an Allende presidency.

> Late Tuesday night (September 15) Ambassador Edward Korry finally received a message from State Department giving him the green light to move in the name of President Nixon. The message gave him maximum authority to do all possible—short of a Dominican Republic-type action—to keep Allende from taking power. . . .
> Ambassador Korry, before getting a go-signal from Foggy Bottom, clearly put his head on the block with his extremely strong message to State. He also, to give him due credit,

started to maneuver with the Christian Democratic, the Radical and National parties and other Chileans—without State authorization—immediately after the election results were known. He has never let up on Frei to the point of telling him to "put his pants on." [9]

On September 29, CIA Director Richard Helms instructed the head of the Clandestine Services Western Hemisphere Division of the CIA, William V. Broe, to arrange a meeting with ITT Vice-President Edward Gerrity.

SENATOR CHURCH. Did you discuss with Mr. Gerrity the feasibility of possible actions by U.S. companies designed to create or accelerate economic instability in Chile?

MR. BROE. I explored with Mr. Gerrity the feasibility of possible actions to apply some economic pressure on Chile; yes, sir.

SENATOR CHURCH. What did you understand the purpose of applying economic pressure to be?

MR. BROE. Well, at that time, September 29, the Christian Democratic Members of Congress were showing indications of swinging their full support to Allende in the belief that they could make a political bargain with him. . . . At the same time, the economic situation had worsened because of the reaction to the Allende election, and there were indications that this was worrying the Christian Democratic Congressmen. There was a thesis that additional deterioration in the economic situation could influence a number of Christian Democratic Congressmen who were planning to vote for Allende. This is what was the thesis.

SENATOR CHURCH. This was the purpose then. Did you discuss with Mr. Gerrity the feasibility of banks not renewing credits or delaying in doing so?

MR. BROE. Yes, sir.

SENATOR CHURCH. Did you discuss with Mr. Gerrity the feasibility of companies dragging their feet in spending money and making deliveries and in shipping spare parts?

MR. BROE. Yes, I did.

SENATOR CHURCH. Did you discuss with Mr. Gerrity the feasibility of creating pressure on savings and loan institutions in Chile so that they would have to shut their doors, thereby creating stronger pressure?

MR. BROE. Yes.

SENATOR CHURCH. Did you discuss with Mr. Gerrity the feasibility of withdrawing all technical help and not promising any technical assistance in the future?

MR. BROE. Yes, sir.[10]

The decision of a significant number of Christian Democratic congressmen to support Allende's confirmation as president, and thus virtually guarantee his election, necessitated prolonging the application of these economic measures. The goals of the CIA and ITT shifted: economic pressures no longer were directed at convincing recalcitrant Christian Democratic congressmen but at activating the military to intervene in political life.

An ITT memorandum from field operatives in Chile, noting the strength of Allende's congressional support, described the more pragmatic option:

> A more realistic hope among those who want to block Allende is that a swiftly deteriorating economy (bank runs, plant bankruptcies, etc.) will touch off a wave of violence resulting in a military coup. . . . Chances of thwarting Allende's assumption of power now are pegged mainly to an economic collapse which is being encouraged by some sectors of the business community and by President Frei himself.[11]

After Allende was assured of congressional confirmation, CIA activities were directed toward encouraging a military takeover by the Chilean armed forces as the remaining viable option. William Merriam, ITT Executive Representative for International Trade, summarized a meeting at CIA headquarters with William Broe: "Approaches continue to be *a Chilean military Leader?*

made to select members of the Armed Forces in an attempt to have them lead some sort of uprising—no success to date." [12] A subsequent ITT memorandum raised the issue of direct U.S. government involvement in a coordinated coup attempt, at the *propitious moment*:

> It is a fact that word was passed to Viaux from Washington to hold back last week. It was felt that he was not adequately prepared, his timing was off, and he should "cool it" for a later, unspecified date. Emissaries pointed out to him that if he moved prematurely and lost, his defeat would be tantamount to a "Bay of Pigs in Chile." As part of the persuasion to delay, Viaux was given oral assurance he would receive material assistance and support from the U.S. and others for a later maneuver. [13]

Realizing that the presidency in Chile would pass to a socialist in November, ITT officials began to elaborate a strategy of external economic coercion designed to lead to internal economic chaos and the ultimate demise of the new government. ITT Chairman Geneen now emphasized that company officials in contact with U.S. government representatives "should demand that U.S. representatives of international banks take a strong stand against any loan to countries expropriating American companies or discriminating against foreign private capital." [14] This strategy was outlined in more detail in an ITT analysis of U.S. policy toward Latin America submitted to Henry Kissinger in late October.

> Inform President Allende that, if his policy requires expropriation of American property, the United States expects speedy compensation in U.S. dollars or convertible foreign currency as required by international law.
>
> Inform him that in the event speedy compensation is not forthcoming, there will be immediate repercussions in official and private circles. This could mean a stoppage of all loans by international banks and U.S. private banks.

Continue the foregoing trend with every possible pressure which might keep Dr. Allende within bounds. . . .

Without informing President Allende, all U.S. aid funds already committed to Chile should be placed in the "under review" status in order that entry of money into Chile is temporarily stopped with a view to a permanent cut-off if necessary. This includes "funds in the pipeline"—"letters of credit." . . .[15]

This strategy was ultimately incorporated into U.S. government policy and became central to the attainment of U.S. policy goals in Chile.[16]

After a period in which U.S. corporations and government officials appeared to be working at cross-purposes and without a clear political perspective (except their desire to undermine the election of Allende), a consensus emerged between Kissinger, the CIA, and ITT. The convergence of views was reached shortly after Allende was confirmed in the presidency: by common consent the strategy consisted of maximizing external economic pressures on the vulnerable points of the Chilean economy, creating political conditions for a coup within a time span longer than that originally envisioned by the early opponents of Allende.

State Dept, CIA & ITT
Cooperation strategy against Allende.

3

The National Security Council and the Initial U.S. Response to Allende

The election of Salvador Allende and the apparent inability of the United States to prevent that outcome was a signal to the Nixon administration of the inadequacy of the foreign-policy-making apparatus. The U.S. executive viewed events in Chile as inextricably bound to developments throughout the region and a direct challenge to U.S. hegemony, already eroded in countries adjoining Chile. Nixon's first response was a statement which outlined his concern with "coherence" and "rationality" in formulating policy toward the region: the multitude of U.S. private economic and political interests had to be brought into order. To correct the organizational deficiencies and to provide the coherence in policy which he sought, several organizational changes were instituted, leading to the formation of a centralized policy-making body capable of coordinating the various threads of U.S. policy. The National Security Council emerged as the crucial policy-making body. It assumed responsibility for devising Chilean policy, and it quickly became apparent that a policy of *political* confrontation had been chosen. The particular issues raised, including nationalization and compensation, were symptomatic of a larger issue: the effort by Chile to break its ties with the United States and seek an alternative to capitalist development. It was that decision and the U.S. opposition which defined the operational meaning of the "political" problem, frequently referred to by high NSC officials, including Kissinger.

In his 1970 foreign policy report to the U.S. Congress, President Nixon dwelled on the need for a special decision-making instrument to deal with critical foreign policy issues and to integrate them into the larger context of long-term U.S. global interests.

> American foreign policy must not be merely the result of a series of piecemeal tactical decisions forced by the pressure of events. If our policy is to embody a coherent vision of the world and a rational conception of America's interests, our specific actions must be the products of rational and deliberate choice. We need a system which forces consideration of problems before they become emergencies, which enables us to make our basic determinations of purpose before being pressed by events, and to mesh policies.[1]

Such an instrument had been in the making since the beginning of the administration, when the decision was made to revive the power of the National Security Council in order that it might "set forth the major foreign policy problems facing the President, discuss the options available to him, and recommend courses of action."[2] A presidential aide described the broad purpose of the Council as one of "anticipat[ing] crises and organiz[ing] options in advance of crises."[3] As a result the "responsibility for coordinating foreign policy planning" passed from Secretary of State William Rogers to the president's advisor on national security affairs and head of the National Security Council, Henry Kissinger.[4]

A series of executive department changes enhanced the stature of the National Security Council in the area of foreign policy and consolidated Kissinger's position as the president's most influential foreign policy advisor. In late 1969, Kissinger was appointed chairman of the newly created Defense Programs Review Committee "whose purpose is to keep the annual defense budget in line with foreign policy objectives." [5] This decision led to a serious weakening of the Secretary of Defense's previously dominant influence over interdepartmental discussions regarding the defense budget. According to a senior Pentagon planner, "the consultation process [was] being formalized and broadened . . . with Henry Kissinger placed in the key post of deciding which issues must be resolved by the President himself." [6] Kissinger was also appointed chairman of two key interdepartmental committees: the Committee of Forty which supervises covert U.S. intelligence operations around the world; and the Senior Review Group which "usually gives final approval to the NSC study memoranda. . . ." [7] In addition, Kissinger chaired the NSC "Washington Special Actions Group" which is "the top level operations center for sudden crises and emergencies. . . ." [8] In 1971, a special intelligence committee under National Security Council leadership was established by President Nixon to review and evaluate global intelligence reports.[9] Hence, Kissinger and the National Security Council were assigned a central role in the shaping of military and intelligence policy as it impinges on overall foreign policy objectives.

Kissinger's immediate response to the Allende electoral victory in September 1970 was to estimate its impact on the hemisphere and to view it as a direct challenge to U.S. economic and political interests in Latin America. He assigned Chile priority status and implied that a short-term or prolonged confrontation between the U.S. and a socialist government in Chile was inevitable. An NSC official described the fundamental difference between the U.S. government assessment of Chile and Peru:

The pattern was not that different with regard to nationalization. . . . The important difference is that in the Peruvian
context you had a different political context. U.S. policy
toward Chile was considered entirely within a much larger
political context and was more important in a political sense,
and was determined to a large extent by political factors.

In the case of Peru, there was a non-constitutional government and policy was largely determined by the IPC [Interna-
tional Petroleum Company] dispute. The copper expropriations were a major factor in Chile, but our relations were still
determined by political factors. When Nixon and Kissinger
assessed Chile after the 1970 election, they were not looking
at it primarily in terms of the expropriation of U.S. copper
companies.[10]

On November 4, 1970, Salvador Allende was inaugurated
as the new president of Chile. The Popular Unity government described Chile as "a dependency of imperialism" and
proposed replacing "the present economic structure, putting
an end to the power of monopolistic capital, both Chilean
and foreign, and also to big landowners, so as to begin the
construction of socialism." [11]

The U.S. reaction was "brusque and frigid," [12] barely
concealing an open hostility. President Nixon outlined the
basis of future U.S.-Chilean relations in his foreign policy
report to Congress in February 1971:

> We deal with governments as they are. Our relations
> depend not on their internal structures or social systems, but
> on actions which affect us and the inter-American system.
>
> The new government in Chile is a clear case in point. The
> 1970 election of a socialist president may have profound
> implications not only for its people but for the inter-American
> system as well. The government's legitimacy is not in ques-
> tion, but its ideology is likely to influence its actions. Chile's
> decision to establish ties with Communist Cuba, contrary to
> the collective policy of the OAS was a challenge to the
> inter-American system. . . .
>
> Our bilateral policy is to keep open the lines of communica-

tion. We will not be the ones to upset traditional relations.
. . . In short, we are prepared to have the kind of relationship
with the Chilean government that it is prepared to have with
us.[13]

Disquiet was expressed in some U.S. congressional quarters
over possible "outright discrimination" by the Chilean
government against U.S. corporate holdings in Chile.[14]

U.S. policy-makers envisaged a definite erosion of U.S.-
Chilean relations in the immediate future. A senior U.S.
policy advisor on Latin America recalled the atmosphere
within U.S. government circles at the time, and the early
application of direct and indirect economic pressures against
the Allende government.

> The election of Allende came as something of a surprise.
> People didn't really believe it would happen. I think there was
> a fairly strong reaction to that election in the White House.
> The concept of a Marxist freely elected. . . . The approach
> taken was essentially to try and keep hands off as much as
> possible, but we certainly weren't interested in being terribly
> helpful to the success of the Allende government. . . .
> Correct but cool. But the expectation was that there would be
> problems because of the kinds of people in the coalition, the
> program of the coalition, the kinds of statements made, and
> the clear intention of nationalizing the copper industry.
>
> Our policy was [characterized] increasingly by a growing
> resentment of economic nationalism, and a feeling that we
> couldn't ignore this. But even with Chile, an attempt was
> made to keep the lines open. Feeling that it was at least
> probable that economic pressures building up because of our
> economic policies and limited access to international agencies
> would either force Allende to compromise or, alternately,
> bring about some change in Chile.[15]

U.S. corporations with investment interests in Chile increased their activity during this initial period. Under the
aegis of ITT, an Ad Hoc Committee on Chile was formed to

apply pressure on the U.S. government "wherever possible to make it clear that a Chilean takeover [of their investments] would not be tolerated without serious repercussions following." [16] The major focus of their efforts was with Henry Kissinger and the National Security Council, and secondarily, within the U.S. Congress. ITT officials were in direct contact with Kissinger's office during January and February 1971 through NSC official Arnold Nachmanoff. According to ITT documents, Nachmanoff, a senior Latin American advisor to Kissinger, told ITT officials that "the best way to get at Chile is through her economy" and "indicated that the U.S. will apply quiet pressure along economic lines and encourage other countries not to invest in Chile." [17] At the initial Ad Hoc Committee meeting in January 1971, it was also argued that "pressure should be brought upon the international lending agencies to cease activity in countries that threaten or actually expropriate private investments whether it is overtly or by 'creeping nationalization.' " [18] ITT representatives at the meeting suggested that the "threat of economic chaos" would have a positive impact on Allende's attitude toward the problems of U.S. corporations in Chile.[19]

The future course of relations between the United States and Chile was clear as early as February 1971. A group of Chilean government officials, headed by the Minister of the Economy, Pedro Vuskovic, visited Washington to argue Chile's case for continued public and private U.S. investment. In the course of discussions, senior U.S. government officials underlined the importance of adequate compensation for expropriated foreign properties. This reflected "the strong pressure on the Administration by United States mining and other private interests whose total investment in Chile [is] estimated at more than $1 billion. . . ." [20] At approximately the same time, President Nixon, with State Department support and at the urging of national security advisor Kissinger, canceled a proposed visit of the U.S.

aircraft carrier *Enterprise* to Chile. Kissinger supposedly argued that the visit would be viewed as a gesture of friendship by the United States toward a Marxist president.[21]

In Chile this decision was criticized by the right-wing opposition who saw the necessity of maintaining close and friendly ties between U.S. military forces and their Chilean counterparts as an essential ingredient in the formula to topple the Allende government. Subsequently the U.S. government "rectified" this tactical error and encouraged military aid, joint exercises, and a substantial U.S. military mission in Chile.

Summary

The National Security Council in consultation and cooperation with an association of large U.S. corporations collaborated in the coordination of a medium-range political strategy to undermine the Allende government. Through their combined efforts they determined the closure of vital financial and economic resources necessary to sustain Chile's dependent economy. The U.S. policy-makers' association with the corporate community and their ability to fashion a common policy was not a fortuitous coincidence but largely reflects the common interests that both share in maintaining Chile within the U.S. sphere of influence. The effort to centralize and rationalize the decision-making structure coincided with the crises in Chilean-U.S. relations and the inadequacy of piecemeal improvised policy responses. By organizational rationalization an effort was made to get on top of events, and to anticipate and shape their direction. The constraints and options that U.S. policy-makers faced in devising a policy for Chile were not only dictated by developments in Chile but by the course of events in the region and especially in Peru and Brazil which in different ways influenced the policy choices of U.S. decision-makers.

4

U.S. Policy Toward Chile in the Context of the Brazilian and Peruvian Models

The Brazilian Alternative

In contrast to the generally hostile response which the election of Allende evoked among U.S. policy-makers, Washington has been exuberant over the behavior and performance of the Brazilian dictatorship: financial resources have been lavished almost without limit. The existence of a pro-U.S. government in Brazil willing to open its markets, resources, and labor to U.S. economic interests and to support U.S. political initiatives was sufficient reason for large, long-term U.S. government financial subsidies to promote U.S. economic exploitation of Brazil. A senior official within the executive branch of the U.S. government recently observed:

> Our relations with Brazil are probably better than with any other Latin American country. From the U.S. point of view, the basis of affinity is the emphasis on our free market forces—an open economy which is a success comparatively speaking and serves as an excellent demonstration of the way we think the world should be run.[1]

Two basic premises underlie U.S. policy toward Brazil: (1) a country the size of a subcontinent with a strong affinity for U.S. capital and dependent on external financing could be a useful strategic ally in maintaining U.S. influence in Latin

America or at the very least maintaining the area within the free market zone; and (2) the political conditions and dimensions of the Brazilian economy and population were such that a meaningful effort could be mounted by the multinationals to promote rapid capital accumulation and expansion based on intensified exploitation of the working class. No other country in Latin America offered the "package" of opportunities available in Brazil and, with the exception of Argentina, none seems capable of providing it. Taking the short view, the United States pursued a policy of promoting its major ally (Brazil), and neutralizing a possible adversary (Peru), as the best way to contain Chile. In other words, the political conjuncture in Latin America at the time of the election of Allende offered opportunities to pursue a relentless policy of encirclement but only when this perspective was tempered by a realistic assessment of the limits imposed by different nonsocialist development efforts emerging in the region.

The U.S. and the 1964 Military Coup

During the early 1960s, Brazil experienced a period of populist government with increasingly nationalist overtones. The administration of João Goulart (1962–1964), moved to expand national control over the country's resources, proposed an income redistribution policy in favor of the lower classes, and attempted to mobilize the latter for organized political action. In the context of a decline in expected rates of profits and a reduction in the rate of total public and private investments (net inflow of private foreign capital dropped from $277 million in 1961 to $70 million in 1963),[2] the Goulart government tried to stimulate the economy by increasing wages while controlling public expenditures and imposing restrictions on foreign capital investment. As a result, the society entered a period of stagnation due to a lack of new investments in the most dynamic sectors of the economy and to the inability of the national alternative, large-scale state investment, to provide a substitute for the drying up of external capital. And, in the midst of severe inflationary pressures, Goulart refused to institute an economic "stabilization" program that would have fallen primarily on wage and salaried workers, although pressured to do so by the U.S. government as a precondition for economic aid. Nevertheless, the Goulart government was not engaged in an effort at profound socioeconomic transformation of Brazilian society. Octavio Ianni has described its reformist and indecisive nature:

> Actually the nationalist model never was an over-all project, since it never came to be formulated in a systematic manner. As a political model for development, distinguished by the rule of the masses, it was structured randomly of occurrences, victories, and obstacles. Some groups and leaders perceived its potentialities but they did not succeed in formulating an over-all project.[3]

The political and economic policies of Goulart had a polarizing effect on the society. Conservative groups drawn from the upper and middle classes organized social and political forces to actively oppose the nationalist leadership. The Brazilian bourgeoisie and petite bourgeoisie felt particularly threatened by the rising political and economic challenge of the lower classes. Within the economic sphere, the petite bourgeoisie were dismayed by the progressive decrease in wage and salary differentials between them and the workers. Under the leadership of the bourgeoisie and U.S. imperialism, the petite bourgeoisie began to move increasingly in the direction of support for a military solution as the only alternative to thwarted ambitions.

> In large part these [the petite bourgeoisie] are the masses that were given opportunities to grow under the administra-

tions of Adhemar de Barros, Janio Quadros, and Carlos
Lacerda. They are ambitious to rise socially at any price.
Their cultural and mental universe is impregnated with
dominant class values and patterns which are spread by
television programs, movies, magazines, and newspapers. For
this reason they see proletarian struggles and claims as a threat
to their ambitions. Consequently they more easily become
attached to the authoritarian solutions presented by some
sectors of the dominant class.[4]

This growing societal conflict was also reflected in the
activities and orientation of the military forces. On the level
of social origins, most of the officer corps were from the
petite bourgeoisie, and gradually the pull of class interests
began to take precedence over any deeply felt adherence to
the norms of constitutional democracy.

Against this backdrop of social conflict and political
instability, the actions of the U.S. government began to
assume a considerable significance. U.S. policy-makers were
concerned with what they perceived to be the increasingly
anticapitalist and procommunist policies of the Goulart
government. They feared the social and political implications of the closure of the Brazilian economy to foreign
investment. Their concern over the possible consequences of
a Goulart administration on U.S. interests in the country was
evident as early as the 1962 nationwide elections. U.S.
sources channeled approximately $20 million into the cam-
paign in support of several hundred anti-Goulart candidates
running for political office (gubernatorial, congressional,
state, and municipal).[5] Beginning in 1963, the U.S. government elaborated a conscious and thought-out strategy which
was designed to bolster the anti-Goulart forces in Brazil,
exacerbate the economic problems of the central government, and, ultimately, bring about the ouster of Goulart. In
a situation where the Brazilian state had ceased to be a
coherent body in which agencies and groups complemented

one another, the U.S. policy became one of disaggregating the state, that is, disaggregating those antagonistic national units (military, middle sector groups, etc.) from a national project, reorienting their allegiances externally, and then moving in concert with these disaffected groups to take over the state and remake it in the interests of the United States and its internal allies. The new state would then serve a new development project.

In pursuit of this strategy, the U.S. government drastically cut back its foreign aid program to Brazil vis-à-vis the central government and successfully sought to influence the international financial institutions in the same direction. During the presidencies of Goulart and his populist predecessor, Janio Quadros (1960–1962), over $600 million in U.S. Agency for International Development loans were approved for Brazil, but over three-quarters of it was not disbursed until after the 1964 military coup.[6] The World Bank supplied no loans or credits to Brazil in 1962, 1963, or 1964, while those provided by the Inter-American Development Bank for the same period totaled only $66 million.[7]

At the same time, the U.S. government adopted a policy of offering economic assistance to selected anti-Goulart groups and individuals, thus increasing the internal pressures on the central government which now lacked the necessary financing for immediate and short-term economic needs. AID was delegated to implement this "islands of sanity" strategy whereby funds were made available and projects undertaken in cooperation with particular state governments, autonomous public agencies, and groups in the private sector. It was "part of a deliberate strategy, to support State governors or regional institutions which were ready to cooperate with the United States in the development of their states or institutions under the Alliance for Progress, and which we thought might be personalities or states (deleted)."[8] Thomas Mann, Assistant Secretary of State for

Inter-American Affairs, outlined the U.S. position in detail before a congressional committee in May 1964.

> We were aware in January by the time I got there—I do not know how much earlier—that the erosion toward communism in Brazil was very rapid. We had, even before I got there, devised a policy to help certain state governments. We did not give any money in balance of payments support, budgetary support, things of that kind, which benefit directly the Central Government of Brazil. This was cut back under Goulart. In my opinion, sir, and I think this is the opinion of many who are informed about Brazil, the fact that we did put our limited amount of aid in the last year of the Goulart administration into states which were headed by good governors we think strengthened democracy.[9]

In assessing U.S. foreign aid policy toward Brazil during the last year of the Goulart government, the U.S. General Accounting Office (GAO) was highly critical of AID for failing "to make dependable technical and economic analyses before making loans," and for "a significant lack of effective administration" in the implementation of numerous capital projects authorized by the agency.[10] AID responded to the GAO report by maintaining that in a situation of political unrest and severe inflation caused by the erratic economic policies of Goulart "realistic financial planning [was] completely unpredictable. . . ."[11] GAO, in turn, dismissed these arguments and criticized the agency's lack of contingency planning even though they were aware of the country's deepening inflation problem at the time the loans were signed.

> We believe that the instances of inadequate planning and project implementation difficulties noted in our review demonstrated that the effectiveness of AID's capital activities in Brazil could have been substantially improved, especially since the potential problems were predictable, to a large degree, at the time the projects were planned or approved.[12]

In the final analysis, AID admitted that loan projects authorized and disbursed before April 1964 were done so on the basis of essentially political and diplomatic, rather than developmental, considerations. To quote the words of the agency itself:

> . . . for overriding U.S. policy considerations, AID undertook a project lending effort. . . . No mention is made of this political and economic setting as the background for AID lending in this period by the GAO.[13]

By January 1964, the U.S. Ambassador to Brazil, Lincoln Gordon, was openly denouncing communist "infiltration" of the Goulart government, and the U.S. embassy in Rio de Janeiro was making itself increasingly accessible to the anti-Goulart forces. The complementarity between U.S. government policy and the interests of U.S. private investors in Brazil appeared, in part, to account for this now open and aggressive collaboration. In December 1963, Goulart declared his intention of engaging in a thorough review of all government concessions held in the mining sector, with a view to canceling all those not in operation during the previous two decades. The U.S. Hanna Mining Corporation's concession in Sao João del Rei was in this category. A more fundamental conflict erupted in the following month when the profit remittance law passed by the Brazilian congress in 1962 was transformed into actual government policy. "[This government] decree settled unequivocally the question, which the law had not made completely clear, of the definition of the capital base on which remittances could be computed. Reinvested profits were to be counted as 'national capital,' not foreign capital, therefore running directly contrary to the oft-stated views of foreign investors and the United States government." [14]

Between January and April 1964, the U.S. government increased its efforts to impose an international financial-credit blockade on the central government of Brazil, in the knowledge that the opposition *golpista* elements—those supporting military coups—were expanding and consolidating their position inside the country. To this end, the United States refused to agree to any major renegotiation of Brazil's foreign debt. The Brazilian government had been pressing for a rescheduling, but the United States, "which held the key to the debt refinancing . . . preferred to follow a waiting game, conceding small short-term renegotiations, but giving no encouragement to Brazilian overtures for large-scale refinancing." [15] The United States refused to enter into negotiations with Brazil until the latter had come to terms with its European creditors who collectively held more of the country's indebtedness than the United States. These negotiations were begun immediately prior to the military coup.

U.S. encouragement to the Brazilian military to move against Goulart came indirectly in the form of a special closed meeting of all U.S. ambassadors, chargés d'affair and chiefs of AID missions in Latin America called by President Johnson in March 1964, less than two weeks before the coup. The meeting was addressed by Thomas Mann, Assistant Secretary of State for Inter-American Affairs and the president's senior advisor on Latin America, who signaled a new, more realistic U.S. approach to nonelected Latin governments, particularly those that displaced democratically elected regimes. Mann was quoted as saying that the United States should modify its opposition to conservative and/or military regimes, and that there would no longer be "good or bad guys" criteria as far as future policy was concerned. [16]

The U.S. labor movement in collaboration with the CIA also played an active role in support of the 1964 military coup, through the AFL-CIO-sponsored American Institute of Free Labor Development (AIFLD), in part a CIA-financed group. On a number of occasions since 1961, AIFLD has infiltrated and used labor movements in Latin

America in the pursuit of overall U.S. policy goals. The most striking instance of U.S. labor involvement in the overthrow of an elected government in Latin America prior to the Brazilian coup was the case of British Guyana in 1963.[17] In the case of Brazil, a substantial number of anti-Goulart trade union leaders were brought to the United States for training and indoctrination. In January 1963, for example, an AIFLD training program for "a special all-Brazilian class of thirty-three participants" began in Washington, in the hope that the participants would return to Brazil and begin to organize the anti-Goulart forces.[18] This they did, and Mr. W. Doherty, Jr., director of the social projects department of the AIFLD at the time of the coup and subsequently administrator of the entire AIFLD operation, has since commented on their key role in the events leading up to Goulart's ouster.

> . . . very frankly, within the limits placed upon them by the administration of João Goulart, when they returned to their respective countries, they were active in organizing workers, and helping unions introduce systems of collective bargaining, and modern concepts of labor-management relations. As a matter of fact, some of them were so active that they became intimately involved in some of the clandestine operations of the revolution before it took place on April 1. What happened in Brazil on April 1 did not just happen—it was planned—and planned months in advance. Many of the trade union leaders—some of whom were actually trained in our institute—were involved in the revolution, and in the overthrow of the Goulart regime.[19]

AIFLD officials were also active in the northeast of Brazil in the precoup period attempting to utilize their resources to accelerate *golpista* tendencies in the rural areas.[20]

The overall U.S. policy toward the Goulart regime was, from the beginning, aggressively hostile. Within a short period of time this hostility had translated itself into a deliberate policy designed to hasten the nationalist government's overthrow. A general policy of disaggregating the Brazilian state was tied to a series of more specific undertakings: the "islands of sanity" strategy; the external economic "squeeze"; financial support and training of internal opposition groups; and the enunciation of a new U.S. policy regarding illegal seizures of political power in Latin America and the installation of military and nonmilitary dictatorships. As the situation deteriorated inside Brazil, these aspects were paralleled by increasingly close and intimate relations between the military and civilian conspirators against Goulart and the U.S. embassy in Rio de Janeiro. U.S. Ambassador Lincoln Gordon was not only a vocal critic of the Goulart regime but apparently actively encouraged the *golpista* elements. Prior to the coup, a representative of the anti-Goulart civilian leadership (made up primarily of business executives and professionals from the state of Sao Paulo) met with Ambassador Gordon to enquire what the U.S. position would be in the event of a protracted civil war. The emissary "reported back that Gordon was cautious and diplomatic, but he left the impression that if the Paulistas could hold out for forty-eight hours they could get U.S. recognition and help." [21] *O Estado de Sao Paulo* described one of the final contacts between the Brazilian military opponents of Goulart and the U.S. embassy before the coup:

> A high official was asked about the possibility of meeting with one of the members of the military section of the Embassy of the United States. He agreed to hold a conversation at the office of the latter. The meeting took place, and on that occasion he received, couched in diplomatic language, an offer of war materials in the case of necessity.[22]

The military coup began on March 31, in the wake of the anti-Goulart "Family's March with God for Freedom" in Sao Paulo, designed to convince high-ranking military officers of the existence of large-scale opposition to the Goulart government. One source has suggested that the military leader, General Humberto Castelo Branco, was finally moved to act by the U.S. military attaché in Rio de Janeiro, General Vernon A. Walters. Walters had strong links with the Brazilian military going back to World War II, when he served as liaison officer with the Brazilian expeditionary forces in Italy. "A week before the coup, Walters wired full details of its organization to Washington, and the day after Castelo Branco was inaugurated as President, lunched with him privately in the Presidential Palace." [23] Further evidence of a direct involvement between U.S. officials in Brazil and the military *golpistas* during the coup itself is presented by the then U.S. Consul General in Sao Paulo, Niles Bond, who has since observed that "our information about what was going on was very good." [24] Bond himself spent March 31 and April 1 "in the office of Adhemar de Barros as the Governor of Sao Paulo was fretting over the indecision of General Amaury Kruel and tracking the progress of his co-conspirators in Minas Gerias and Guanabara." [25]

The U.S. government responded to the success of the military coup with a mixture of ecstasy and relief. It was in the words of one U.S. official "a big change for the better." [26] President Johnson conveyed his own unqualified support for the coup in a message sent to the new provisional president of Brazil, Ranieri Mazzilli, within twelve hours of the latter's installation:

> Please accept my warmest good wishes on your installation as President of the United States of Brazil. The American people have watched with anxiety the political and economic difficulties through which your great nation has been passing, and have admired the resolute will of the Brazilian community to resolve these difficulties within a framework of constitutional democracy and without civil strife. [27]

The chairman of the Senate Subcommittee on Latin America, Wayne Morse, called Johnson's message "a beautiful statement . . ." and declared his complete support for the "constitutional" (!) transfer of power in Brazil.

> . . . the developments in Brazil did not result from action by a military junta or from a coup by a military junta. Instead, the overthrow of the presidency of Brazil resulted from developments in which the Congress of Brazil, acting under Constitution of Brazil, was the guiding force, and was reinforced by a military group which backed up the preservation of the Brazilian constitutional system.[28]

Nothing illustrates the bankruptcy of U.S. liberalism better than Morse's response. Congressmen were arrested, unions outlawed, strikers arrested, political opponents by the thousands were interred, tortured, and killed, yet we are informed that the coup was accomplished to preserve "the constitutional system." In a speech to the Brazilian National War College, U.S. Ambassador Gordon saw the coup taking its place "alongside the initiation of the Marshall Plan, the ending of the Berlin blockade, the defeat of Communist aggression in Korea, and the solution of the Cuban missile crisis as one of the critical points of inflection in mid-twentieth-century world history." [29] He later told a congressional committee that the change in government "had to come about if there were any chances of preserving democracy in Brazil." [30] The rhetoric about "preserving democracy" was later dropped as world public opinion gained knowledge of the repressive nature of the regime; U.S. apologists then turned toward the economic side of the junta's activities to justify the dictatorship.

The U.S. role in the events leading up to the coup was a critical factor in its ultimate success. Nonetheless, U.S. policy-makers have subsequently propounded the view that the Goulart government "fell largely from the weight of its own ineptitude." [31] This position was echoed by the U.S.

business community whose combined economic investment in Brazil at the time of the coup was estimated at $1.5 billion. They explained the internal economic deterioration primarily in terms of "the irresponsible policies of the military government's incompetent predecessor" and were, according to *Business Week*, "tremendously relieved" at Goulart's demise.[32]

The parallel between the methods, arguments, and goals in the U.S. effort to overthrow Goulart and the military coup that overturned the Allende government are striking.

The United States and the Military Dictatorship

The Castelo Branco government quickly moved to restore foreign business confidence in Brazil, so much so that by the end of 1965 *Business International* could declare that "the present Brazilian Government has taken just about every necessary step to allure new foreign investment. . . ."[33] The profit remittance law was amended in a number of important respects: the registration of foreign investment capital could now be made in the country of origin; restrictions on profit remittances were eliminated, except in the event of a major balance of payments crisis; reinvested profits reverted to being "foreign capital"; and the period of tax benefits and assistance was extended. The military dictatorship agreed to compensate the American Light and Foreign Company for properties nationalized by the Goulart regime and sought to encourage private capital to exploit the country's iron-ore reserves and to play a vital role in the expansion of the petrochemical industry. Various foreign companies, including the Hanna Mining Corporation, gained new concessions. It was also proposed that the National Motor Industry be sold to private interests and that a policy of cooperation between Petrobas and the foreign oil companies be implemented. Two further government decisions were also designed to weaken the role of the state in the industrial sector of the economy. First, it issued a decree canceling the proposed expropriation of Brazil's six private oil refineries announced (but not carried out), by Goulart in March 1964. Second, it reactivated that section of the Capital Market Law "permitting the sale to private investors of part, or in some cases all, of the state-owned investment in federal mixed-capital companies." [34] The military also granted extremely favorable terms to U.S. imports financed under AID loans, in the form of a minimum guarantee deposit of only 25 percent (compared with a normal deposit of 50 percent), and no requirement for prior import deposit or exchange surcharge. "These concessions [to U.S. imports] have now been granted in respect of all imports financed by foreign loans at a term of 20 years or more, but this would appear to be a valueless concession to virtually all exporters outside the USA." [35] In addition, the Castelo Branco administration signed an investment guarantee treaty with the U.S. government.

The new Brazilian regime, in effect, began to broaden the basis for Brazilian dependence. On the one hand, they continued to cut back on public expenditures, thus making increasingly precarious the position of many national firms dependent on government financing. This, in turn, facilitated the foreign capital takeover of "inefficient" national enterprises. On the other hand, the government embarked on a deliberate policy of attracting foreign capital and integrating it with state capital. The state would provide the infrastructural assistance, guarantee the security of foreign capital and the existence of a cheap labor force. Instead of a development strategy based on the redistribution of income to the lower classes, the new policies were rooted, in part, in depressing and strictly controlling wages and reconcentrating income in favor of the upper and middle groups in society, and in the formation of internal markets based on these groups.

The U.S. government and the international financial institutions were ready and willing to provide large-scale economic assistance to the anticommunist military junta. Within days of the coup, the Inter-American Development Bank approved a number of loans to Brazil "which the United States' director had earlier been prepared to veto or delay." [36] In June, the U.S. government made an emergency $50 million loan to the junta "at the unusually low interest of two percent. . . ." [37] This loan was instrumental in giving the new government an aura of respectability for upcoming negotiations on rescheduling of the country's foreign debt. On July 2, the United States, Japan, and Brazil's Western European creditors agreed to reschedule 70 percent of the medium-term commitments due for repayment in 1964 and 1965. This decision involved more than half of Brazil's approximately $3 billion foreign debt (of which $1.3 billion was owed to the United States), and was an important factor in allowing the generals more breathing space to deal with the most immediate and pressing economic problems.[38] In December, the U.S. government signed a $375 million aid agreement with Brazil as part of an estimated $1 billion program in support of the country's economic development activities in the following year. Approximately $450 million of the total amount was to be provided by the International Monetary Fund, the World Bank, the U.S. Export-Import Bank, other private banks, and private Brazilian creditors in the United States and Europe.[39] Such assistance played a major role in creating the infrastructure for future capitalist development and growth in Brazil.

Confidence in the capacities of the military junta was also expressed within the U.S. business community now that "pro-Western leaders with pro-Western ideas are in power," [40] even though the initial response by foreign investors in general was somewhat cautious and reserved. We have already noted their enthusiasm over the coup and the pro-foreign-investment orientation of the new government. Nonetheless, they were anxious to see just how the junta's policies would be applied in practice. This early reticence also reflected another important concern: the restoration of economic stability and growth potentialities which the initial influx of large-scale economic assistance from the United States and the multilateral agencies was designed to bring about.

Throughout the administrations of Castelo Branco (1964–1967), and Costa e Silva (1967–1969), Brazil was the recipient of more external economic aid than any other country in Latin America. The massive commitments announced at the end of 1964, which included two $125 million standby credits from the IMF, culminated in a World Bank decision in 1968 to make available up to $1 billion in loans to the military dictatorship for projects to be undertaken in the transport, power, industrial, mining, and educational sectors of the economy.[41] Paralleling these developments was a pronounced increase in the flow of foreign private capital into the country, following the wait-and-see attitude of the first year of the new government. Between 1966 and 1968, total foreign investments (including reinvested earnings) amounted to $1.25 billion.[42] U.S. investors accounted for a large proportion of this total. If we consider the four year period 1965 to 1968, we find that U.S. private investors poured $635.1 million directly into Brazil, and a further $78 million via base companies in Panama, Netherlands, Antilles, and the Bahamas.[43] Short-term investor caution over a government "practically made to order for foreign investors"[44] was soon transformed into active involvement in a development process geared to the need for external capital and conducive to profit maximization.

In the years immediately following the 1964 coup, the

largest portion of U.S. foreign aid to Brazil was channeled through the Agency for International Development. By the end of 1968, AID had administered approximately $1 billion in support of development projects in various sectors of the economy.[45] However, AID-funded undertakings continued, much as during the Goulart period, to be subject to faulty planning and inadequate implementation. A congressional study mission to Brazil in late 1966 encountered numerous instances "where AID projects had bogged down or were demonstrations of wasteful inefficiency" in part because of "insufficient surveillance or carelessness on the part of AID officials. . . ."[46] In their highly critical report on AID activities in Brazil, the study mission pointed to the problems confronting a water supply improvement project in the state of Bahia undertaken by the agency in collaboration with the Inter-American Development Bank, and quoted comments from AID in Brazil to buttress its case.

> Planning and coordination for this project appears to have been deficient. Installation of the main source pipeline is still delayed two years; expansion of the distribution system is still incomplete. Total costs for the project were seriously underestimated. Field coordination between USAID and IDB representatives was difficult. Only a few joint contacts were made at the job site. Often USAID representatives in Recife were not informed of IDB visits to Salvador in time to coordinate activities. Had IDB representatives been on the spot to observe and deal with unanticipated problems, it is probable that pipeline construction could have progressed faster and more effectively.[47]

A General Accounting Office study of U.S. aid to Brazilian education (focusing primarily on the post-1968 period) described a similar situation of inadequate information and lax planning.

> The program managers administering U.S. bilateral education projects in Brazil generally do not have sufficient

information to make adequate analysis of proposed and ongoing education projects undertaken by the international assistance agencies. Consequently, it is extremely difficult, if not impossible, for these U.S. officials to fully assess whether the projects, substantially supported with U.S. funds, are consistent with Brazil's education priorities and investments as well as with U.S. bilateral education programs.[48]

The GAO study concluded that U.S. aid to the Brazilian education system had "directly and indirectly" reinforced the prevailing distortions within the system: "Our review showed that U.S. education assistance efforts were not designed to improve the inequities in the Brazilian system, including inequitable distribution of education opportunities between urban and rural areas and disparity in education spending between the affluent and poor areas." [49] Clearly, such observations provide a strong justification for arguing that political considerations continued to be the main rationale behind AID policy. U.S. AID policy was geared to strengthen the dominant social classes, to fasten their control over the social life of the country while contributing to widening the inequalities within society.

Since 1964, the U.S. government has provided over $2 billion in economic and military assistance to the right-wing military dictatorship in Brazil in support of a political environment conducive to U.S. economic penetration. Stuart H. Van Dyke, Director of the AID mission in Brazil, in testimony before a House subcommittee in 1968, alluded to the political nature of U.S. economic assistance in the following exchange, after being pressed by the subcommittee in regard to the overwhelming U.S. support for Brazil since the 1964 coup.

MR. RUMSFELD. Do you have anything to justify your conclusion [that the U.S. decision to strongly support the military government was correct]? I do not see that it followed logically, necessarily, and there is nothing to go with it. It is just hanging there.

MR. VAN DYKE. It is just a statement of how we view the immediate past in Brazil. The change was a desirable one— the change in 1964.

MR. RUMSFELD. I am not challenging that.

MR. VAN DYKE. But our support was essential—I should say "essential"—our support was desirable in order to prop up. . . .[50]

The thrust of U.S. policy is also sharply delineated in a discussion between Van Dyke's successor as director of the U.S. AID mission in Brazil, William A. Ellis, and the chairman of the Senate Subcommittee on Western Hemisphere Affairs during congressional hearings on Brazil in 1971:

SENATOR CHURCH. How does the present government, in which we have invested $2 billion, serve the national interests of the United States, in your judgement?

MR. ELLIS. Well, first of all, perhaps I should state what I think some of the U.S. national interests are in Brazil. One of them is the existence of a government or society which is generally consistent with our national, specific national, security interests in the hemisphere which would not pose a security threat to us. Second would be the protection and expansion, if possible, of our economic interests, trade, and investment in the hemisphere.

SENATOR CHURCH. Can you tell me how large the American private investment is in Brazil today?

MR. ELLIS. It is somewhat over $1.6 billion.

SENATOR CHURCH. So we have pumped in $2 billion since 1964 to protect a favorable climate of investment that amounts to about $1.6 billion.

MR. ELLIS. That is only one of the objectives, Mr. Chairman.

SENATOR CHURCH. I want to get these things in relation. We have spent $2 billion on a program one objective of which is the protection of a favorable investment climate for private business interests in this country.

MR. ELLIS. Yes.[51]

U.S. direct and indirect external assistance is even more strikingly revealed if we consider the period 1969–1972, when total external assistance authorized to Brazil from all sources was in excess of $2 billion. These sources included the World Bank ($877.3 million), the Inter-American Development Bank ($592 million), the Export-Import Bank ($458.4 million), the International Finance Corporation ($56.3 million), and various United Nations organizations ($20.1 million).[52] U.S. support of multilateral assistance to Brazil during this three year period stands in sharp contrast to its policy regarding multilateral aid for Peru and Chile.

The critical role of U.S. economic assistance in consolidating the anticommunist military dictatorship has, over time (especially since 1968), allowed the United States to contract its lines of credit and to occasionally criticize particular aspects of the junta's economic policies without in any way endangering the junta's position.[53] In 1973, total U.S. economic aid to Brazil amounted to only $53.8 million.[54] However, the slack has been enthusiastically taken up, as the above figures suggest, by U.S.-influenced "international" financial agencies. According to a senior economist of the World Bank, Brazil has become "a kind of *enfant cher* of the Bank," while an official of the Inter-American Development Bank called Brazil "the only country [in Latin America] that is really moving ahead. They have projects, projects, projects." [55] These two institutions gave a combined total of $313.9 million in loans and credits to Brazil in 1973.[56]

The "flexible and pragmatic" [57] policies of the military government in Brazil have, from the point of view of the foreign investor, more than counterbalanced the problem of a persistently high level of inflation, which has remained in the vicinity of 20 percent annually since 1967.[58] The profits of forty-six leading firms surveyed by *Business Latin America* in 1969 increased by an average of 74 percent over 1968. In 1970, the average profits of these same firms was up 67 percent over 1969.[59] Included in the enterprises surveyed were the U.S. affiliates of General Electric, Standard Oil, Ford, Texaco, Bethlehem, Chrysler, Union Carbide, Firestone, Goodyear, and North American Rockwell. In fact, during 1970 the average profitability of U.S. investments declined in every Latin American country with the exception of Brazil, where they experienced a 28 percent increase in earnings and a 13 percent increase in book value, resulting in an increased rate of return of 11.2 percent compared with 9.8 percent in 1969.[60] In a period of resurgent economic nationalism in Latin America, manifesting itself in increasing demands for national controls over resource industries and restrictions on foreign investment, Brazil's attractiveness to the foreign investor, in spite of price controls and the relatively high cost of credit, was only too evident. The First National City Bank of New York put it this way:

> At a time when doors are closing to foreign investors all over South America, Brazil has boldly staked its future on an open economy.[61]

Between 1970 and 1972, over $1 billion in new direct private foreign investment and reinvestment was registered with the Central Bank of Brazil.[62] Total direct U.S. private investment stood at over $2 billion.[63] Profits continued at their previous high levels during 1971 and 1972, according to *Business Latin America*. The average corporate profits of private and state-owned companies surveyed in 1971 rose 64 percent and in the following year increased by 67 percent. The return on net worth (capital plus reserves), averaged 16 percent and 18.5 percent respectively.[64] The effects of inflation were minimized by the government's application of monetary correction and price adjustment systems. The investment climate in Brazil exceeded "even the wildest dreams of international investors" [65] and continued to do so notwithstanding government moves to restrict foreign borrowings, introduce more stringent controls over the operations of foreign companies, eliminate a number of fiscal incentives, and push for more Brazilian equity participation in foreign enterprises. These actions represented, not a reaction to large-scale foreign capital penetration, but an attempt to diversify Brazil's sources of financial dependence within the international capitalist system, a dependence which has increased with each passing year. The increasing role of West Germany and Japan in the Brazilian economy has allowed Brazil to reorient and generalize her dependence on international capitalism.

Although the new Geisal administration has raised the possibility of a future foreign investment code in Brazil, this has been coupled with a recommendation "that Brazil's policy of 'fair—even favorable' treatment of foreign capital remain unchanged." [66] In the hope of improving on the $1 billion in foreign investments and loans that entered the country in 1973, the government decided to end the policy of requiring a 40 percent deposit on new foreign loans, beginning in 1974.[67] Major incentives to foreign investors continue to overshadow attempts to control their activities. Despite a worsening inflation problem (which reached 50 percent during the early months of 1974 and is expected to average 35 percent for this year),[68] these inducements have combined with a political climate based on repression and social policies designed to intensify the exploitation of labor, hold down the socioeconomic demands of the lower classes and effectively marginate them from participation in society, to make Brazil an ideal location for foreign investment. Or, in the words of an influential U.S. analyst of business conditions in Latin America: "Overwhelmingly, Brazil still looks extremely good to international firms." [69]

Although we have argued that Brazil has developed a more generalized economic dependence on a number of capitalist countries in recent years, as distinct from specific dependence on a single capitalist country (e.g., the United States), it must be emphasized that the United States continues to retain its political and military pre-eminence vis-à-vis Brazil. The U.S. government has worked to consolidate the military junta's internal position and to encourage the junta's hegemonic ambitions within Latin America. The most explicit example of the latter was President Nixon's statement to General Medici in 1971 that Brazil's future direction would have a decisive impact on the rest of the hemisphere.

U.S.-Brazilian military relations have been particularly close since 1964 due, in part, to long-standing personal relationships between U.S. military personnel and a number of the junta generals, stretching back to World War II. A senior U.S. military officer involved with Latin American affairs has observed:

> Our military relations with Brazil are very close. Our relations with Brazil go far back. There was cooperation during World War II. Much of the leadership today in Brazil is made up of World War II veterans. This is the basis of our relations. Service-to-service and army-to-army relations are outstanding, couldn't be better.[70]

The U.S. has played a key role in securing the military junta's internal position and its capacity to control insurgent movements. Direct U.S. military assistance, the training of Brazilian military officers in the United States, and a U.S. public safety program in Brazil between 1959 and 1972 which was the largest in Latin America and provided training (direct and indirect) for 267,000 officers and police personnel has helped to all but eliminate any serious threats to "internal security." [71] In fact, by 1970, U.S. military assistance to Brazil was being scaled down because, to quote from the report of a special congressional mission to that country:

> It is clear to the study mission that Brazil is at least one place in the hemisphere where U.S. assistance has helped the armed forces of a country to reach a point of self-sufficiency, thereby allowing the phasing out of certain functions and a reduction in its mission personnel.[72]

Nonetheless, U.S. military personnel with whom the mission spoke uniformly emphasized "the continued importance of the military assistance training program as a means of exerting U.S. influence and retaining the current pro-U.S. attitude of the Brazilian Armed Forces." [73] For U.S. policy-makers, however, Brazil's military and economic strength has elevated it to a position where it can play an important role in the furtherance of U.S. policy goals in the hemisphere. Brazil is now viewed as a base for the political, economic, and military penetration of other countries in the region. The following comment by a U.S. military officer with responsibility for politico-military affairs in Latin America is quite specific on this point:

> On the diplomatic–foreign affairs level, it is obvious that Brazil is going to be the United States of Latin America. Due to their economic progress, they can now assist Latin American countries economically and politically. They have given a great deal of aid to Bolivia. Brazil is in a position to be more responsive to sensitive military requests from [the new military government in] Chile. We weren't about to send Chile tear-gas stuff.[74]

U.S. policy toward Brazil has been premised on two basic interrelated themes. First, satisfactory relations with Brazil have been viewed as essential to the overall long-term policy goals of the U.S. in Latin America.

Certainly a definite desire on the part of Nixon and the administration to maintain good relations with Brazil. Essentially a geopolitical view. You simply could not allow relations with a country the size and significance of Brazil to deteriorate badly and expect to have a constructive relationship with Latin America. Specific issues caused problems, for example, the fisheries problem and coffee. But these were worked out in a practical sense so that major conflicts were avoided. . . . In retrospect, the will to resolve differences with Brazil was so strong at the highest levels on both sides, that they were resolved to at least avoid confrontations over fisheries and coffee issues.[75]

Second, U.S. policy-makers have responded favorably to the Brazilian development strategy, based on foreign multi-national corporate investment, political repression of the lower classes, the reconcentration of wealth in the hands of the upper class and a developing consumer-oriented middle class. Assistant Secretary of State for Inter-American Affairs Charles Meyer summed up the U.S. attitude: "We consider that Brazil is a country whose developmental record has been—well, it is statistical [sic], the development record has been transcendental." [76] Some policy-makers have attempted to rationalize the repressive aspects of the development process by reference to national character explanations. "No one condones the repression. The problem is that Brazilian authorities have always acted brutally toward the people. That is, there is no political newness to the idea of beating someone with a club. Unfortunately, an old Brazilian habit." [77]

A more commonplace response has been, on the one hand, to minimize the extent of the repression and, on the other, to focus on its positive aspects, viz., its contribution to the creation of political control of the lower class and a suitable climate for foreign investment and profit maximization. This view is discussed in detail by a State Department official whose involvement with post-1964 U.S. policy toward Brazil has been considerable.

> If you are talking about censorship and the loss of complete political freedom, torture of prisoners, this does go on to some extent. Much of the censorship is self-administered. A good bit of tolerance in it. Not our way, but in a way legitimate. Don't want energies/efforts of the country diverted. I don't feel that development is taking place by oppressing any people and sweating it out of the people by having them tighten their belts. Development is taking place applying classical economics, with sensitivity to good communication between government and business sectors and agricultural sectors. Feeling is that economic growth is clearly the overall objective of the country. They are doing it with good economic policies, they stimulate investment, they let investment be rewarded, exceptional profit opportunities.
>
> Most Brazilians are apathetic to censorship and torture. They are pretty satisfied with the way things are going. They have provided a certain amount of stability in the political/social situation. Don't see parades broken up on the streets, don't have riots, terrorist groups broken up, greater feeling of calm.[78]

Nor could the impact of the socialist government in Chile be discounted in any discussion of the evolution of U.S. policy toward Brazil in the early 1970s. A senior U.S. policy advisor on Latin America, while dismissing any "explicit" attempt to build up Brazil as a counterweight to Chile within the hemisphere, agreed, however, that this consideration was "certainly a factor" in the minds of policy-makers. "[They] considered Brazil in the context of Latin America and a Marxist Chile." [79]

The Peruvian Alternative

In 1968, a military coup took place in Peru, triggered in part by the incapacity of the reformist Belaunde government to carry out social and economic policies that would undercut the possibilities of social revolution emerging as a real option in the early and middle sixties. The new military government evinced an interest in elaborating a program for dynamic capitalist-industrial development in Peru, and to this end they embarked on a strategy designed to shift the locus of economic power away from the traditional agricultural and banking elites, toward new modern industrial entrepreneurial elites. In the process, they engaged in a policy of selective reforms and sectoral nationalism. Certain industries and enterprises (such as International Petroleum Company) were nationalized while others remained in private hands. However, this nationalization was not incompatible with private foreign and domestic capital investment. Nationalizations continued to be accompanied by new concessions to private investors. Foreign investment was welcome provided it adhered to the new "rules of the economic game" (profit reinvestment and remittances, specific sectors of the economy closed to new foreign investment, etc.), as outlined by the military government.

During the period 1969 to 1971, U.S. policy-makers adopted a position of hostility toward the governing military junta in Peru, over the latter's seizure or expropriation of properties belonging to U.S. multinational corporations such as Standard Oil of New Jersey, W. R. Grace Company, and Gulf Oil Corporation. A top U.S. policy-maker explained the relationship between business and U.S. policy in the following manner:

> The United States Government has declared a responsibility to protect the legitimate interests of American investors overseas. . . . In the particular case of Peru the United States policy is one of reasonableness. We seek and indeed insist that the Government of Peru give prompt, adequate, and effective compensation for the properties and assets which it has, in the exercise of its sovereign power, taken.[80]

In effect the U.S. government was assuming the right to determine Peru's development priorities, arguing that scarce foreign exchange earnings be diverted away from development projects toward paying U.S. corporations. It should be noted here that prior to 1968, according to an influential U.S. business analyst, "Peru's official attitude toward foreign investment was similar to and even more 'hands off' than her Latin American neighbors. . . ."[81]

U.S. bilateral aid to Peru was reduced and U.S. influence within the international financial institutions was successful in drastically affecting the flow of multilateral economic assistance to the military government. Treasury Under-Secretary Walker admitted that a relationship existed between the cutting off of Inter-American Development Bank funds for approximately two years and the expropriation (without compensation) of International Petroleum Company (IPC) in 1968.[82]

Nonetheless, the overall U.S. response reflected a certain degree of ambivalence regarding Peru's economic nationalism. A former high-ranking U.S. policy advisor on Latin America within the National Security Council recalled the divergent interdepartmental positions:

> My feeling was that Peru represented a significant, perhaps even a positive, evolution in Latin America and one we could work with if we could not allow IPC to override the entire relationship. . . . On the whole, the relationship was better than it might have been if certain interest groups and elements had been predominant within the structure of the U.S. government, that is, people who pushed sanctions and the hard-line. The hard-liners were primarily State Department lawyers, the Defense Department. . . . The NSC staff tended to be softer-lined on Peru. We argued for, and continued to push for, avoiding allowing the economic issues to override the larger political relationship. Some in the State Department also favored that. The Secretary of State tended to be harder-lined than some of his staff people.[83]

Unlike the case of Chile, expropriations in Peru were not intended to result in a socialist transformation but to modify Peru's terms of dependency and to provide a basis for industrialization with the inclusion of foreign capital. Dominant policy-makers distinguished between changes *within* capitalist property relations in Peru (the shift from a laissez faire agro-mineral export society dependent on the United States to a statist industrializing society with a variety of sources of external finance: "diversified" dependency), and changes *away* from capitalism in Chile. This important *political* distinction was the basis for making the issue of nationalization of U.S. property in one instance negotiable and in the other a point of confrontation.

Beginning in late 1971, a visible change in U.S. policy to Peru began to take shape. The decision was the result of the convergence of a number of factors: "the proven durability and stability" [84] of the military government; its domestic anticommunism, and a development strategy of capitalist modernization-from-above combined with restricted mass mobilization from below; compensation settlements with W. R. Grace and Gulf Oil and only limited restrictions on profit remittances abroad; continuing negotiations on the IPC issue; and, in general, what one State Department official called "a reassessment [by Peru] of the role of foreign investment." [85] Economically, the Peruvian military government continued to control and limit the role of foreign capital within a mixed economy. However, these constraints and further nationalizations were accompanied by new concessions to foreign capital. Major U.S. and foreign oil companies signed a number of new exploration contracts with the junta, and increasing foreign participation was evidenced in new industrial and mining undertakings. Peruvian economic nationalism was concerned with redefining, not eliminating, dependence on foreign investment. This fact was clearly understood by the U.S. Ambassador to Peru,

Taylor Belcher, and his arguments in support of renewed
U.S. economic aid to Peru had a considerable impact within
the councils of the U.S. government. "Ambassador Belcher
argued that, with the Peruvian government carrying out
ambitious investment programs, there was considerable business to be done here by American companies—but that they
had little chance if the U.S. government restricted Peruvian
access to international financing." [86]

The findings of a World Bank economic mission to
Peru in late 1972 and early 1973 concurred with the
U.S. ambassador's view, and deserve to be quoted in some
detail:

> . . . while a number of industrial activities have been
> declared as "basic" and reserved for the state, generous fiscal
> incentives are being given to private investment and activity in
> the rest of the industrial field. Similarly, while the increased
> control over the credit market is being used to influence the
> allocation of credit, there is no evidence that shortage of
> credit has restricted private sector activity. Neither has the
> introduction of complete government control over imports so
> far resulted in restrictions on imports of capital or intermedi-
> ate goods needed for industrial expansion.
>
> An equally flexible policy has been followed concerning the
> admission of foreign capital in Peru and the regulation of its
> operation. The strategy of reconciling national aspirations
> with need for foreign direct investment is well illustrated also
> by the contract arrangements under which a large number of
> foreign oil companies have started exploration and drilling
> operations in Peru in the recent period. . . . The government
> at the end of 1971 took action to facilitate foreign participa-
> tion in joint ventures for industrial activities. Finally, it has
> also availed itself of the escape clause of Resolution 24 of the
> Cartagena Agreement [Andean Pact], which permits the
> supplying of domestic credit to enterprises classified as foreign
> under that resolution.[87]

A further consideration in the thinking of U.S. policy-makers was the emergence of a socialist government in Chile. One former U.S. ambassador to Latin America characterized the "new flexibility" toward Peru as part of a policy designed to isolate Chile from the rest of the hemisphere.[88] Another senior policy-maker suggested that this strategy was an important factor in U.S. government deliberations: "We clearly saw from the beginning a distinction between Peru and Chile, [this is] how we felt about events then affecting our interests." [89]

Indicative of this changing policy was an increasing tendency to separate specific conflicts involving U.S. investor interests and to support the view "that Peru had a significance larger and more important than the [particular] investment dispute." [90] Under-Secretary of State for Security Assistance Curtis W. Tarr elaborated on this shift in emphasis:

> We have disagreements, obviously, with respect to fishing rights, but this does not mean that across-the-board, we disagree with the Peruvians. It does not mean that our relationships on that one point alone are absolutely sour. The American contacts with Peru are considerably more extensive than those that are affected, either by their seizure of plants or by the seizure of our fishing boats. At a time when Peru was actually seizing some of our corporate assets, there were other American corporations who were investing in Peru.[91]

In June 1973, U.S. Secretary of State William Rogers made an official visit to Peru and declared the U.S. government's support for the military junta's "constructive nationalism," [92] even though compensation for expropriated U.S. properties (IPC and W. R. Grace), remained outstanding. Within the hemispheric and international financial agencies, the U.S. government moved to support multilateral loans and credits to Peru. In August–September 1973 it voted in favor of two Inter-American Development Bank loans to

Peru totaling $35.6 million and one World Bank loan of $25 million for agricultural development.[93] *Business Latin America* offered a provocative explanation of this new U.S. policy:

> The reasons behind the United States change of heart are not entirely clear. Peru is a potentially important source of oil and minerals and the United States may feel it is not the best of policies to alienate this cornucopia at a time when the developed world is vying for key raw materials. Also, with the social revolution in Chile falling apart, the United States may feel less threatened in Latin America and more willing to accept Peru as it is and deal with the country on its own terms.[94]

Two senior economists in the World Bank with responsibilities in the Latin American section agreed that the United States had exercised leverage in respect of the bank's policy toward Peru. One commented that the $25 million loan in August 1973 reflected, in part, a "weakening" of the U.S. position regarding the settlement of outstanding investment disputes,[95] while the other described the explicit nature of the prior U.S. pressure to forestall World Bank loans and credits to Peru.

> The World Bank is very friendly to Peru at the moment. There was a frost as long as the United States objected to Peru because of the expropriations. This has now been fixed up. If McNamara had wanted to he could have said to the U.S., "Fuck you, we are going ahead anyway. We have enough votes. Therefore, fuck you." But his Achilles Heel was the IDA [International Development Association] replenishment, which depended on the U.S. Congress. Since the staff of the World Bank and the IDA are one it really makes the whole thing dependent. The World Bank message from the White House and the Treasury was "If you go ahead against our wishes [and make loans to Peru] we will try and screw up our next IDA replenishment." [96]

These actions coincided with a U.S. decision to resume direct negotiations with Peru in an attempt to resolve a series of disputes involving U.S.-owned properties which had been nationalized without compensation. James R. Greene, Senior Vice-President of Manufacturers Hanover Trust Company, was designated by President Nixon to act as his personal representative to the Peruvian government. The subsequent nationalization of a subsidiary of the U.S. Cerro Corporation did not affect the status of these negotiations because of a Peruvian willingness to discuss the question of compensation.[97] The agreement that emerged had both short-term and long-term consequences. It accommodated the immediate Peruvian position, while increasing the country's long-term indebtedness to the United States. In essence, the United States, through the First National Bank of Boston, agreed to extend $150 million in loans to Peru, $74 million of which was to be paid directly to five nationalized U.S. companies (Cerro Corporation, W. R. Grace and Company, the Starkist Foods subsidiary of the H. J. Heinz Company, Goldkist, Inc., and Cargill, Inc.). The International Petroleum Company was conspicuously missing from this list. The other $76 million was to be paid to the U.S. government for distribution to other U.S. companies whose assets were nationalized by the Peruvian military government.[98] A concern of U.S. policy-makers in pushing for a package settlement was "to defuse the situation in order to open up Peru and its mineral and oil wealth again for United States investors." [99] This willingness "to settle outstanding problems with the United States" was an important factor in the decision of the World Bank consultative group on Peru to commit over $1.9 billion in external financing over a three year period beginning in early 1974.[100]

"U.S. policy toward Peru," observed a U.S. policy advisor, "has developed surprisingly well. The one contentious issue is

IPC. But other than that, there seems to be a disposition on
the part of the Peruvians to take an amicable posture toward
the United States on some issues. There is no overt hostility.
In the United States, there is a feeling that the Peruvian
model is certainly preferable to the Chilean model." [101]

The emergence of a socialist government in Chile had a
significant impact on U.S. policies toward Peru and Brazil:

> Chile helped make it possible to keep open the relationship
> with Peru and to avoid the problems with Brazil. The concern
> over Chile governed by a Marxist government led people
> within the U.S. government to feel that it was more important
> than they realized to maintain constructive relations with the
> Latin American countries.[102]

In the wake of the Chilean coup, one U.S. policy-maker was
led to declare:

> The Peruvians came around because of the Chilean change.
> We are now in a position to take a much tougher position
> toward other [Latin American] countries now that we have
> eliminated a major problem.[103]

The Brazilian and Peruvian Alternatives: A Conclusion

The existence of democratic-socialist Chile forced the
United States to come to terms with Peruvian nationalism.
The United States preferred to accept limited nationalizations that contributed to stabilizing a regime supportive of a
mixed economy than to risk radicalizing the situation in Peru
through confrontation tactics. Beginning in early 1971 the
United States realized that the nationalist measures in Chile
could strengthen political forces in Peru which were pressur-
ing for a more rapid and thorough transformation. To
continue its intransigent policy of economic pressure without

any substantial access points in the regime (in contrast to Chile) would provide the Peruvians with no option but to take measures following the Chilean pattern.

Brazil and Peru appeared to represent alternative capitalist development models to the Chilean. In Brazil it appears that the emphasis is on promoting foreign investment to stimulate industrialization while in Peru the emphasis appears to be on state capital. However, a closer examination would reveal that Peruvian development is more comparable to an earlier period of Brazilian development during which the state undertook to promote a series of investment projects in heavy industry, infrastructure, and natural resource development. It could be the case that Peruvian statism is merely laying the groundwork for a later period in which the door will be opened for large-scale foreign investment. Certainly the decisions taken by the junta do not preclude that future option. And it appears that U.S. policy is premised on that possibility, leaving aside the investment possibilities that exist even today. In any case, during the late 1960s and early 1970s U.S. policy-makers were greatly influenced by what they described as the successful economic growth pattern in Brazil. The capacity of the regime to hold down wages and to effectively exclude nationalist and trade union activities facilitated the process of private accumulation and capital expansion by the multinational corporations. While the Brazilian experience presented itself to U.S. policy-makers as a model for Latin America, Brazil served as an active base of political support of U.S. policies in Chile.[104] Thus, while U.S. policy was directed at containing Peruvian nationalism within the boundaries of a mixed economy and limiting Peru's political ties with Chile, in Brazil the United States sought to promote Brazilian expansionism and to increase its ties with Chilean opposition groups and military officials. Hence the United States' concern with Chile caused it to accommodate Peruvian nationalism and to expand its commitments and ties with Brazil. And, while the United States sought to influence events in Chile, it was influenced by experiences in Brazil: the logic of these political developments was the effort to transplant to Chile the experience in Brazil.

5

Foreign Economic Policy, the Copper Conflict, and the Foreign Debt

The Blockade of Chile

The existence of alternative capitalist development poles to the Chilean strengthened U.S. efforts to thwart its socialist experiment. In addition, however, there were two other basic considerations which have to be taken into account in analyzing U.S. policy. The growth of economic competition from Western and Eastern Europe, Japan, China, and the U.S.S.R. offered Latin American countries the possibility (over the medium run), of diversifying their sources of external finance and subsequently weakening both their economic ties and dependence on the United States and the latter's political influence in the area. The second consideration pertained to the influence which Chilean development might have on other countries within the region, what was described by numerous influential officials variously as the ripple or domino effect: a successful effort by Chile would encourage economic nationalists elsewhere. Conversely, if the Chilean experience could be induced to fail, the United States and its apologists could write and argue about the "failures" of socialism. Under conditions of growing competition, in which it appears the United States was losing ground, U.S. policy-makers may have felt that their hegemonic position in the region could no longer be maintained by strictly economic relations, but that there was a need to promote strict and direct political control through a dependent military regime. The efforts to bolster the sagging fortunes of U.S. economic interests in the face of external competition and internal threats resulted in the establishment of the Council on International Economic Policy, an organization which fitted in nicely with President Nixon's desire for a rational and coherent foreign policy approach based on long-term structural developments.

The U.S. government's negative response to the election of Allende in September 1970, rooted in a conflict of political and economic interests, crystalized into specific policies shortly thereafter. The White House and the National Security Council settled on an overall strategy of controlled escalation of hostile measures in which periods of conflict would alternate with periods of negotiation. This strategy involved the combining of a two-pronged attack: prolonged economic confrontation and the gradual disaggregation of the Chilean state. The tactics designed to realize economic dislocation in Chile were essentially threefold: an international credit squeeze, via mobilization of support for the U.S. position within the international financial institutions and amongst Chile's international creditors; the elaboration of an ideology of "lack of creditworthiness" based on conditions (inflation, disinvestment, etc.) created, in large part, by the U.S. credit blockade; and the identification of gradual economic deterioration with internal government policy, thus creating the economic basis for polarizing Chilean society in a manner favorable to the groups of owners of large properties. These efforts were paralleled by the deepening of ties between the United States and critical sectors of the Chilean state (military, police), and private institutions (employer associations). In the process, these groups were separated from the executive branch and its national project and mobilized in support of U.S. policy goals. The U.S. government's strategy of a gradual accumulation of internal forces stood in opposition to the initial more narrowly conceived responses of certain U.S. corporations (ITT, etc.), with major economic investments in Chile. As one official in the National Security Council told us:

> A major consideration, both in general expropriation policy and in the case of Chile, was that it is all very well to go in and support one company, but the costs involved in going into Chile would be very high . . . no country should sacrifice its overall relations or interests or other groups in the country for the sake of one interest group.[1]

U.S. policy-makers continued to cloak their policies in the rhetoric of moderation and compromise and to express public interest in negotiations with the Allende government aimed at resolving outstanding differences. However a high CIA official noted a different aspect of the negotiating posture: ". . . our intelligence requirements in the [debt] negotiations between the United States and Chile, would be to try and find out, through our sources, what their reactions to a negotiating session were, what their reading of our position was, what their assessment of the state of negotiations is."[2] U.S. policy-makers claimed "a real effort to avoid a direct confrontation," "an unwavering willingness on our part to take the extra step," "continuous negotiating," and to be "keep[ing] the door open."[3] In point of fact, however, this professed desire for negotiations was but a tactical element in the overall U.S. strategy. It was designed to allow time for the economic squeeze to gradually engender a general societal deterioration, and direct military intervention in the political arena. In a secret memorandum to the State Department in early 1971, U.S. Ambassador Nathaniel Davis emphasized that a military coup would only occur when public opposition to the Allende government became

."so overwhelming, and discontent so great, that military intervention is overwhelmingly invited." [4]

The National Security Council, while maintaining overall responsibility for policy toward Chile ("Chile's an NSC matter," said one U.S. official [5]), delegated the application of specific measures to the appropriate government agencies. This delegation of authority allowed NSC officials to mediate between different agencies and departments over the specific measures adopted to implement policy. The NSC sought to maximize pressure in Chile but without forcing a premature rupture in relations (i.e., before a coup could be consummated). One NSC official described the tactical infighting and their own role in the following terms:

> NSC input has generally been on the side of counseling a more moderate approach to dealing with these countries. This puts us in the middle of a number of fires. The Treasury takes a hard line on expropriations and the president takes a very hard line too. The State Department takes a very cautious line—traditional—in dealing with these problems. The NSC point of view leans toward the State point of view. . . .
>
> Treasury was very hard-line, and had a strong input but their views were not dissimilar from those of the president because Connally and the president talked a lot. The State Department line was more moderate, although it would have condoned nothing. NSC was pretty much in the middle. Our general feeling was "let's keep the doors open." The position followed came out quite similar to the NSC position.[6]

These interdepartmental differences of opinion were primarily different appreciations and estimates of the most effective mix between external coercion and internal pressure as means of realizing the desired changes in Chile and Latin America.

In January 1971, at the suggestion of NSC advisor Henry Kissinger, President Nixon established a Council on International Economic Policy (CIEP) to "provide a clear, top-level focus on international economic issues and achieve consistency between international and domestic economic policy." [7] It represented a decision on the part of the U.S. government that "economic interests cut directly across foreign policy considerations and thus bear on military and diplomatic commitments abroad." [8] One of the purposes envisaged in establishing the council was "protecting and improving the earnings of foreign investments." [9] The newly appointed director of CIEP, Peter Peterson, outlined the basis of the new foreign economic policy in a study requested by the president.

> The tradition of the Yankee trader, which we may proudly invoke, is a tradition that placed its faith in more trade, not less. And now that others have become first rate economic powers in their own right, there must also be the realization that political, economic and security questions are inseparable in long-range policy planning, and that it is the global relationships which in the end must be protected and nurtured. In an increasingly economic, interdependent and competitive era, we shall also find increasingly that economics is politics.[10]

An NSC staff member was more concise: "We are willing now to push harder on economic interests. . . ." [11] A key policy-maker in the implementation of this new policy was Secretary of the Treasury John Connally, whose "unparalleled" [12] influence with President Nixon enabled him to reassert Treasury's pre-eminence in the making of foreign policy as it affected international economic policy and vice versa. He utilized his position as chairman of the National Advisory Council on International Monetary and Financial Policies, which is charged with recommending what position the U.S. government should take on loan requests from the international financial institutions, to make Treasury "slightly more equal than the others on close votes." [13] Furthermore, the U.S. executive directors on the boards of the World Bank, Inter-American Development Bank, and the International Development Association were Treasury officials, directly answerable to the Secretary of Treasury.

The close convergence of government policy and business interests was made evident in the response to a decision by Ecuador to expropriate the property of All American Cables and Radio, a subsidiary of International Telephone and Telegraph (ITT). The Ecuadorian government offered ITT $575,000 in compensation as against the latter's demand for $600,000. The corporation then proceeded to pressure the U.S. government to invoke sanctions and withhold all future economic assistance to Ecuador until the ITT demand had been met. "ITT was determined to teach the Ecuadorians a lesson as a matter of principle," one U.S. official observed. "They were trying to teach all of Latin America a lesson." These actions were successful, largely because, according to this official, the Treasury Department "adopted the ITT position uncritically." [14]

The U.S. government refused to accept new loan applications from Ecuador during most of 1971, and a $15.8 million AID authorization was held up until a settlement was reached with ITT. In the Inter-American Development Bank, the United States was able to forestall approval of three loans to Ecuador totaling $21.5 million until after the conflict had been resolved in favor of ITT. "According to sources in Washington well informed about U.S. economic policy in South America, the Ecuador case was important because it served notice that the United States would not flinch from invoking sanctions even when a token sum of money was involved. It represented a solid victory for Treasury Department hardliners." [15]

Testimony before congressional committees by high-ranking Treasury officials underscored the decisive role of the department in the formulation and execution of foreign economic policy. "Developing countries," declared Charles E. Walker, Under-Secretary of the Treasury, "must . . . tread very lightly in using expropriation of foreign investments unless there is evidence that satisfactory progress is being made toward settlement of expropriation disputes." [16] During the first half of 1971, the United States abstained from voting on a World Bank livestock loan for Bolivia over the question of compensation for expropriated U.S. properties.

> . . . despite settlement of the Gulf Oil dispute, other expropriations have taken place and evidence is as yet insufficient to conclude that progress toward compensation is being made. A parallel position was taken on an Inter-American Development Bank loan to Bolivia related to the World Bank loan.[17]

In June, the U.S. executive director to the World Bank, Robert E. Wieczorowiski, abstained from voting on a $6 million loan to Guyana for flood control, contending that it was too early to make a judgment on the progress of compensation negotiations between the Guyanese government and a recently nationalized Canadian bauxite corporation (ALCAN), with substantial U.S. ownership.

MR. REUSS. Did the President of the World Bank indicate a position as to whether this proposed loan to Guyana should go forward in that it was accompanied by evidence that progress was being made toward the resolution of the ALCAN expropriations?

MR. WIECZOROWISKI. There was not what you would call a formal provision of evidence but I think it was clear that in bringing the project forward there was a determination on the Bank's part that this policy was being met.

MR. REUSS. Did you abstain on your own or did the Secretary of the Treasury instruct you to?

MR. WIECZOROWISKI. My actions within the World Bank group do have the guidance of the Treasury and the NAC (National Advisory Council) and I was acting with such guidance.

MR. REUSS. And their guidance was to tell you to abstain.

MR. WIECZOROWISKI. Yes, sir.[18]

The loan was supported by the other twenty members of the World Bank board, including the Canadian representative. One Treasury policy-maker explained the U.S. decision in these words: "When we directed an abstention or negative vote on Guyana, we were concerned that if Guyana followed through on its bauxite nationalization there would be a wave of nationalizations sweeping the Caribbean. [Nationalization activities setting a precedent] was our long-run concern, particularly in the Andean nations and in the Caribbean." [19]

Before the House Subcommittee on Inter-American Affairs, John R. Petty, Assistant Secretary of the Treasury for International Affairs, maintained that the U.S. position on compensation payments for expropriated U.S.-owned properties was consonant with long-standing World Bank policy. He questioned "the policy of the Bank in lending when there were unresolved expropriatory issues outstanding." The United States' vote with respect to Guyana was "a signal to the management of the World Bank that we thought that administration of the policy wasn't quite the way we read the cards." He concluded with an explicit statement of the U.S. position:

> . . . there is an appropriate place for a policy where the U.S. government can support the activities of its nationals abroad through a fair and balanced policy of deterrents, indicating that there are economic costs involved in expropriation for the host country, and that if they seek to pursue their policy, the costs will be incurred.[20]

The U.S. government was opposed, not merely to expropriation without adequate compensation, but to the very principle of nationalization itself.

In an interview with *Business Week*, Secretary of the Treasury Connally was quoted as saying that "the U.S. can afford to be tough with Latin Americans because we have no friends left there anymore." [21] The statement was later retracted; its importance lies not in what it tells us about Latin America (where the U.S. could count on Brazil, Paraguay, and Central America among others as "friends"), but about the state of mind of U.S. officials. The wish to appear "isolated," the garrison mentality, was a convenient way of justifying an arbitrary and unilateral policy conceived to support exclusively narrow U.S. economic interests. Hence the U.S. policy of economic pressure against Allende's Chile was part of a larger regional policy of general opposition to all efforts at autonomous national economic development, a policy which, as we have seen in the case of Peru, was later modified.

U.S. economic pressure on the Allende government, in the form of declining government, private banking, and commercial credits, began immediately following the 1970 election. U.S. policy was less a response to specific sector nationalizations than to the more fundamental political and economic issues raised by the fact that a thorough socialist transformation was envisioned in Chile. The economic conflicts were the immediate sources of conflict for these more basic considerations. While keeping this in mind it is important, however, to follow the sequence of events that led to confrontation.

On September 29, 1971, Allende announced that $774 million would be deducted as excess profits from any compensation due the Anaconda Company and Kennecott Copper Corporation for the nationalization of their Chilean assets.[22] Since most estimates placed the book value of the nationalized mines at $500 to $600 million, the "no compensation" decision by the controller general of Chile was not unexpected.

U.S. policy-makers, with increasing support from influential congressional quarters, reacted angrily to the Chilean actions. They left little doubt that a forthcoming presidential policy statement would reflect the hardened U.S. position on the treatment of foreign governments who nationalized U.S. investment assets without adequate compensation. A broadside against the Chilean action was soon leveled by influential U.S. officials. "Obviously in some cases our interests may outweigh the effects of expropriation," said one U.S. official. "But generally, countries that expropriate our assets will be on notice that this will generate a fresh policy review at very high levels of government." [23] Concern was expressed that a "soft" response to this problem would serve to encourage further expropriations, especially in Africa and Latin America. Robert S. McNamara, President of the World Bank and former U.S. Secretary of Defense, declared his support of the U.S. position in some pointed remarks to the International Center for Settlement of Investment Disputes. "[He] warned developing countries that a 'disquieting' trend by governments to annul agreements with foreign investors could 'seriously imperil' their creditworthiness and inhibit investment in their entire region." [24]

U.S. Secretary of State William Rogers, in an official government response, charged Chile with making a "serious departure from accepted standards of international law" in employing the excess profits concept. In a crude attempt to induce global pressures on Chile, he then threatened to reduce the general level of U.S. aid to the underdeveloped world: "[Chile's] course of action . . . could have an adverse effect on the international development process." [25] Assistant Secretary of State for Inter-American Affairs Charles Meyer also attacked "the retroactive application of the 'excess profits' concept" and reiterated U.S. insistence on "just compensation for expropriated properties." [26] The excess profits concept was used by U.S. policy-makers to differentiate between Chile and Peru:

> There is a difference of degree between our problems in Chile and our problems in Peru. For example, the Chilean government has enunciated the Allende doctrine which permits them to unilaterally determine whether a given company has made excess profits in the past and deduct those profits from the value of the nationalized property. This is an extreme departure with a number of implications around the world.
>
> Peru didn't charge excess profits [and] their criteria is different, and much less difficult in terms of international law, in that they say that the arbitration provisions under which Standard Oil operated there were faulty. This is a lot different from saying "You made too much money and we are going to take it away from you." None of the other cases in Peru are remotely comparable. But at least the principle of compensation is recognized in Peru, with the exception of IPC, as compared to Chile.[27]

U.S. corporate interests responded in a similar vein. The excess profits statement signified that "the issue [was] no longer simply between the companies and Chile but between Washington and Santiago." [28] In October, the executives of six U.S. corporations with holdings in Chile (Anaconda, Ford Motor Company, First National City Bank, Bank of America, Ralston Purina, and ITT), met with Secretary of State Rogers for " 'an open discussion' of their predicament and the possible response of their government." [29] Rogers opened the meeting by stating that "the Nixon Administration was a 'business Administration' in favor of business and its mission was to protect business," [30] and voiced concern that Chile's actions could have a domino effect throughout Latin America in the absence of strong U.S. retaliatory action. He also raised the issue of an informal embargo on spare parts and

materials being shipped to Chile and, according to some
reports, told the corporation executives that the U.S. government intended to invoke the Hickenlooper Amendment and
eliminate all aid to Chile unless the expropriated copper
companies received swift and adequate compensation. The
Treasury Department, meanwhile, was attempting to formu-
late a ruling (through the Internal Revenue Service) whereby
the copper companies would be granted a $175 million tax
deduction on their copper losses in Chile.[31]

During September and October 1971, ITT elaborated in
detail on possible U.S. government policy options in dealing
with the Allende government. In a memorandum that
proposed the formation of a special NSC task force to put
pressure on Chile, the following actions were suggested:

1. Continue loan restrictions in the international banks such
   as those the Export-Import Bank has already exhibited.
2. Quietly have large U.S. private banks do the same.
3. Confer with foreign banking sources with the same thing in
   mind.
4. Delay buying (copper) from Chile over the next six
   months.
5. Bring about a scarcity of U.S. dollars in Chile.
6. Discuss with CIA how it can assist the six month squeeze.
7. Get to reliable sources within the Chilean military.[32]

A revised version of the ITT 1970 "White Paper" on Chile
discussed possible State Department actions:

1. Exercise the United States veto in the Inter-American
   Development Bank with respect to several Chile loan
   applications with the bank.
2. Through use of U.S. veto or pressure, shut off any pending
   or future World Bank loans to Chile.
3. Continue the refusal of the U.S. Export-Import Bank to
   grant any loans to Chile.
4. Indicate the State Department's strong displeasure with

Chile's flagrant disregard for norms of international law in nationalization without adequate compensation and urge the U.S. banking community to refrain from extending any further credits to Chile. If possible, extend this to international banking circles.

5. Halt all AID projects that are still in the government pipelines.

6. Embargo imports from Chile into the United States. (Value of Chile exports to the U.S. now is about $154 million.)

7. Enlist the support of Chile's neighbors, particularly Argentina, Brazil and Peru (and possibly Bolivia with its new rightist government) to protest in international forums about the reported offer of arms credits to Chile by the Soviet Union. . . .[33]

Having deleted the more extreme aspects of their earlier proposals, the proposed ITT strategy converged with U.S. government policy and practice.

The political-economic nature of the U.S. credit blockade of Chile between 1970 and 1973 was sharply delineated in an exchange between the Assistant Secretary of the Treasury for International Affairs, John Hennessy, and the Chairman of the Senate Subcommittee on Multinational Corporations, Frank Church, during hearings on the efforts of International Telephone and Telegraph to overthrow the Allende government in 1970 and 1971. Questioned on the immediate termination of credits by U.S. government agencies and the multilateral development institutions to the new Chilean government, Hennessy maintained that these decisions were typically made when new governments came into office whose purpose was to induce "far-reaching new economic programs" or "a whole new structural approach":

SENATOR CHURCH. I do not mean to belabor the point, but there have been instances where credit is immediately extended to a new government, not only by our own agencies but by the multilateral institutions. I have in mind what happened in Bolivia, when credit was immediately made available. It is not always necessarily the pattern to wait and see what the Government is going to do before giving credit.

MR. HENNESSY. The distinction I am making, the difference here is when far-reaching new economic programs, when a whole new structural approach is about to be undertaken, and at the same time statements are being made about their international obligations, that there are going to be expropriations—those types of things raise doubts in the mind of any banker, and I am sure in the case of these banks' management.[34]

Between 1964 and 1970, over $1 billion in economic assistance flowed into Chile from the U.S. Agency for International Development, the U.S. Export-Import Bank, the World Bank, and the Inter-American Development Bank. During the same period, $200 to $300 million in short-term lines of commercial credit was continuously available to Chile from U.S. private banks. Almost 80 percent of all short-term credits came from U.S. suppliers and U.S. banks.[35] Throughout the Allende government's tenure, aid disbursements to Chile from U.S. AID, the U.S. Export-Import Bank, the World Bank (IBRD), and the Inter-American Development Bank (IDB), were nonexistent or negligible, while short-term lines of credit from U.S. private banks declined to around $30 million. The virtual elimination of long-term development loans from AID, IDB, and IBRD, together with increasing demands for the immediate repayment of debt obligations incurred by the Alessandri and Frei governments, constricted the opportunities for long-term development, planning, and investment. The decline in short-term credits drastically affected Chile's capacity to import adequate quantities of essential goods for the day to day operation of society, and over time affected the standard of living and economic productivity of the country.

In August 1971, the Export-Import Bank informed the Chilean ambassador in Washington that any further loans or guarantees from that institution would be dependent on a satisfactory resolution of the copper conflict.[36] It also terminated all loan guarantees to U.S. commercial banks and exporters engaged in business activities in Chile, as well as "disbursements of direct loans that had been previously negotiated by the Frei government. . . ." [37] The withdrawal of the commercial and political risk insurance program was directly responsible for the erosion of short-term U.S. private bank and supplier credits.

The role of the White House, and presumably NSC, in these actions was apparently decisive in view of a further incident involving the Export-Import Bank and Chile at this time. Eximbank Chairman Henry Kearns announced in June that a pending loan request by Chile to finance the purchase of three U.S. Boeing passenger jets had been denied because of the lack of proper assurances on compensation for the expropriated U.S. copper companies.[38] A Department of Commerce official termed the decision basically political in nature, and minimized the importance of Chile's credit standing as a factor in the outcome. Although the State Department questioned the likely effect of this decision on current negotiations involving other U.S. interests in Chile, and on "delicate negotiations elsewhere in Latin America, notably Venezuela," [39] the White House–Treasury position was upheld. State Department officials contended privately that the final decision to refuse the loan "was made on 'the White House level' under the pressure of private American companies." [40]

The U.S. government also displayed a high profile within the multilateral aid institutions, particularly the Inter-American Development Bank and the World Bank. With the exception of two educational loans totaling $11.6 million to the Austral and Catholic universities, both opposition educational strongholds, the IDB awarded no long-term development loans to the Allende government. A $30 million loan application for the construction of a petrochemical complex was shelved after the U.S. executive director voiced strong objections to a bank plan to send a technical mission to Chile to evaluate the request.[41] According to an official of the Inter-American Committee on the Alliance for Progress (CIAP), the United States employed a number of tactics in an effort to hold up IDB loans to the Allende government.

> The U.S. had the opportunity in the IDB to hold up loans. The pressure could go through different channels: (1) veto power. But the problem is to get a more sophisticated way of holding up loans; (2) either by using the power you have in the subcommissions of the Board—the technical way; [or] (3) the political way—calling the director of this department and telling him what you think. At least the last two methods were used.[42]

A similar situation prevailed in the World Bank which did not make a single loan to the Allende government despite the fact that a number of detailed projects were submitted for consideration. In one instance, an appraisal mission to Chile to evaluate a fruit-processing plant project (part of the agrarian reform program and considered crucial in improving Chile's balance of payments situation), was canceled at the request of the State Department.[43] Nevertheless, Chile continued to meet its debt service obligations to the bank. At the 1972 annual meeting of the board of governors of the World Bank, the Chilean representative, Alfonso Inostroza, observed that disbursements from loans approved in the pre-Allende period were approximately equal to Chile's payments to the bank. "If no fresh credits are granted to us," he continued, "the time will come when Chile's debt service payments to the Bank exceed the sums which it received from it. The paradox would then come to pass of Chile becoming a net exporter of capital to the World Bank, instead of the Bank assisting Chile." [44] A World Bank official, in assessing the Allende period, rationalized the institution's credit embargo in the following manner:

> During the Allende period, the World Bank followed the same attitude as the Russians. The World Bank had an economic mission in Chile in 1971, as did the Soviets. Both had the same ideas. As Fidel Castro put it, "this is a revolution of consumption, not investment." The World Bank response was, in bourgeois terms, that unless the investment-savings rate goes up the Allende government is not interested in economic growth and development. Same position as the Russians. The Allende government told the World Bank to go to hell because they were bourgeois economists. They said the same thing to the Russians—that they were going the Chilean way. Therefore, Chile received no help from the Soviet Union and very little from us. The Chileans really went wild. [45]

In October 1971, a congressional subcommittee inquired of Treasury Under-Secretary Walker as to what the U.S. position within the World Bank or the Inter-American Development Bank would be in response to a loan request from the Allende government:

> I would put it within the context of an expropriation of property in which there has been absolutely no indication up to this time that the compensation will be adequate or timely. On that basis if a loan to Chile were to come up today in the Inter-American Development Bank or the World Bank—the World Bank has a rule and they would not lend to Chile under these circumstances, but the IDB has no such rule—there is no doubt in my mind what Secretary Connally's instructions to Mr. Constanzo [U.S. executive director] would be. . . . [46]

The role of the International Monetary Fund with regard

to Chile was somewhat more ambiguous. While the IMF, like the World Bank, conditions aid on a country's general economic policies, officials of the institution "are more willing than they were in the past to recognize that their short-term exigencies can have adverse effects on long-term policies and that they ought to take these effects into account in the demands they make on countries wanting to use the fund's resources." [47] Under the presidency of Pierre-Paul Schweitzer, the IMF has been prepared to admit "that its economic demands often were politically unacceptable to governments caught in the exigencies of development." [48] In the case of Chile, the IMF helped prepare the country's debt renegotiation brief and resisted the U.S. position that Chile accept a standby agreement. IMF loans to Chile of $39.5 million and $42.8 million from the export compensation fund in 1971 and 1972 partly reflected the fact that the fund "is not a bank but a mechanism to assist member-countries with foreign exchange difficulties; moreover, since the Fund had clear authority to make compensatory loans for this type of foreign exchange shortfall, the United States did not object." [49] But, perhaps more importantly, the European members of the IMF appear to have a relatively greater impact on its policies vis-à-vis the United States as compared with their leverage within the World Bank. A U.S. attempt to replace Schweitzer as president of the IMF was vigorously, and successfully, opposed by the Latin American and European members of the fund. Nevertheless, the partial defeat for the United States in the International Monetary Fund over the question of Chile needs to be put in perspective. The IMF only provided Chile with loans for very specific and limited purposes. Long-term development-assistance credits remained dependent on the acceptance of austerity IMF standby agreements, which would have limited the Allende government's internal economic autonomy and had a negative impact on the standard of living of the working class, the major social basis of support for the government.

The cumulative impact of U.S. economic pressures on the Chilean economy led to a severe economic deterioration by early 1973, and allowed the United States to justify a continued credit squeeze on the basis of Chile's supposed lack of creditworthiness, a situation which previous U.S. policy was designed to bring about. During 1971 and 1972, however (before the effects of the credit squeeze set in), the Allende government's economic policies compared more than favorably with those of the reformist Frei administration. According to a study by the Inter-American Committee on the Alliance for Progress, a major accomplishment of the Allende government was the elimination of economic stagnation and the achievement of "a more equitable distribution of the benefits of economic growth. . . ." [50] After analyzing the government's policies through 1972, the study concluded on the following note:

In 1972, the country's economy is in a situation of almost full utilization of its productive capacity, following a year marked by high growth levels. Unemployment has been reduced markedly and a broad process of redistribution of income and accelerated agrarian reform has been carried out.[51]

Nevertheless, the study also issued a warning:

According to Secretariat estimates, relief in the payment of service of the debt over the next few years will be necessary in order to maintain an adequate growth rate over that period. Furthermore, if the prospects for copper prices do not change, the estimated growth in the volume of exports will not be sufficient for generating resources for balancing the balance of payments current account.[52]

Chilean attempts to cope with economic problems resulting from U.S. pressures took the form of a nonconfrontation strategy based on alternative sources of financing and new trading partners. Although Chile was able to renegotiate $300 million in debts to foreign governments and private creditors and obtain $600 million in credits and loans from socialist bloc countries and Western sources in 1972, many of these loans and credits "[were] tied to specific development projects and [could] be used only gradually." [53] The situation was also affected by the precipitous decline in Chile's foreign exchange reserves, resulting from the fact that approximately one-third of the country's total export earnings in 1970, 1971, and 1972 [54] went to service the foreign debt, at a time of rising import prices, increasing domestic demand, declining world copper prices, no U.S. credits, and the refusal of the U.S. government (Chile's major creditor) to renegotiate Chile's public debt to the United States. Finally, U.S. suppliers were now demanding "cash in advance for essential raw materials and parts sales to Chile." [55] Chile's efforts were ultimately not adequate to the situation: the country could not at one and the same time meet both past external obligations and current economic pressures and develop the economy.

In January 1972, President Nixon outlined a stringent U.S. public position on expropriations, which was intended to define the U.S. position on Chile and Latin America. While acknowledging the State Department's concern with U.S. global foreign policy interests, the statement noted the "re-emergence of the Treasury Department as a central and undisguised directing force in international economic policy." [56] It began by questioning "the wisdom of any expropriation . . . even when adequate compensation is paid," and continued:

. . . when a country expropriates a significant U.S. interest without making reasonable provision for such compensation to U.S. citizens, we will presume that the United States will not extend new bilateral economic benefits to the expropriating country unless and until it is determined that the country is taking reasonable steps to provide adequate compensation or that there are major factors affecting U.S. interests which require continuance of all or part of these benefits.

On the face of the expropriatory circumstances just described, we will presume that the United States Government will withhold its support from loans under consideration in multilateral development banks.[57]

This policy statement provided the legal justification for the Treasury Department's activities since 1969 in pursuit of larger U.S. policy goals. "Before the January 1972 statement was made public," a Treasury official pointed out, "Treasury was already following that position. Treasury had already been applying that policy." He described specific examples:

The State Department opposed abstaining on the Guyana vote. This was the Treasury position. On Bolivia in 1971 the U.S. abstained. In the Inter-American Development Bank in 1969, the U.S. abstained on Peru. The director said to us that the U.S. abstained to show its displeasure. The policy statement was a kind of clarification put down on paper. That was more or less the Connally influence, hard-line, that in the case of expropriation, the United States would vote no, or would show its displeasure regarding the proposed loan by, at least, abstaining.[58]

The State Department sought to interpret the new policy directive as "a compromise" but one in which "Treasury got the better part of the deal." [59] Some Treasury officials tended to concur with this view:

Secretary Connally did play a key role. He had input directly with Kissinger and the president. He had the policy role with respect to the multilateral financing institutions. But he was not having, by any means, the final word. On the other hand, when the battle was going on between Treasury and State, we won on the expropriation statement and got it out and published. On the other hand, the surveillance group to keep an eye on the expropriations and carry through the policy was put under the control of the State Department.[60]

Presidential assistant and Executive Director of CIEP (Council on International Economic Policy) Peter Peterson stated that the hard-line policy was designed to provide "investment security" for U.S. investment capital in the underdeveloped world.[61] Sectors of the U.S. business community, however, disputed this contention, viewing the policy as short-sighted and potentially counterproductive. They expressed concern over its possible effect on the entire investment climate in Latin America, and felt that any application of the sanctions policy to a particular country would eliminate the likelihood of compensation for previously expropriated companies there. They also raised the specter of the U.S. investor being denied complete access to those countries subject to the sanctions.

> For example, to the extent that U.S. bilateral aid and multilateral aid and multilateral assistance is choked off, and other countries including the USSR and Eastern Europe are invited to fill the gap, U.S. suppliers and investors may find themselves needlessly cut off from a market.[62]

Finally, it was argued that the expropriation threat was essentially limited to one country, Chile, which was no longer a recipient of U.S. economic assistance.

> By strengthening a policy which fits a situation that is the exception rather than the rule, it could be argued that President Nixon is overresponding and perhaps taking an action which in itself does a basic disservice to the investment climate. It tends to make the investment situation throughout Latin America look infinitely worse than it is.[63]

The criticisms of the corporate interests were based not on a rejection of the principles enunciated by Nixon but on their applicability to Latin America, a Latin America which they perceived as open and receptive to U.S. capital.

The businessmen saw no need to elaborate a general policy statement about Latin America when the issue at hand was the specific problems affecting U.S. relations with one country: Chile. The thrust of the Nixon policy was clearly aimed at increasing the external pressures on the socialist government of Chile, in order to exacerbate internal economic disorder and social conflict and to lessen the attractiveness of the Chilean model to its neighbors. U.S. policymakers perceived Chile as the linchpin in the Latin American struggle to redefine its political and economic relationships with the United States.

A former NSC staff member with responsibility for Latin America, commenting on the situation in August 1973, approximately one month before the military coup, admitted that U.S. policy was geared for a major confrontation:

> . . . to adopt a policy where virtually every investment dispute escalated into a government to government dispute was wrong. That is pretty much where we are right now. It would be difficult for us to isolate investment-expropriation issues from political issues. . . . I think it is very difficult for Allende to work out a solution which the U.S. government could ever consider a reasonable one.[64]

In March 1972, following the January policy statement on expropriation, the Nixon administration vigorously supported passage of the Gonzalez Amendment by the U.S. Congress. The amendment required the president to instruct the U.S. executive directors in the various multilateral aid institutions to vote against loans or the utilization of funds for any country which (1) nationalized or expropriated U.S.-owned properties; (2) declared invalid existing agreements with U.S. corporations; or (3) applied discriminatory taxes or other operational restrictions effectively resulting in nationalization or expropriation. Only presidential determination that an arrangement for satisfactory compensation has been made, or that the dispute has been submitted to the rules of the Convention for the Settlement of Investment Disputes for arbitration, or that "good faith negotiations are in progress aimed at providing prompt, adequate, and effective compensation under the applicable principles of international law" could prevent implementation of this high profile policy within the international institutions.[65]

In August 1973, a Treasury Department official assessed the results of this active interventionist policy.

> We find that the United States has been rather successful in blocking those loans [to countries that have expropriated U.S. properties]. But there is a difference between the Inter-American Development Bank and the World Bank. In the World Bank, the management decides what loans should be brought up to the board of directors. But if the management decides not to bring up the loan, then it doesn't come to a vote. In that sense, I don't know how many loans were turned down because the U.S. view announced it would oppose them. But in the Inter-American Development Bank, the management can bring loans to a vote of the board of directors and the countries themselves can do the same. But realizing that loans would be voted down if they were brought up, they have not been requested to be voted upon by the interested country. In that sense, the policy has been more effective than we believed that it was.[66]

In an address to the 1973 annual meeting of the World Bank and the International Monetary Fund in Nairobi, Kenya, U.S. Treasury Secretary George Shultz restated the hard-line U.S. position: ". . . we do not find it reasonable that a nation taking confiscatory steps toward investment that it has already accepted from abroad should anticipate official assistance, bilateral or multilateral." [67] During a subsequent appearance before a U.S. congressional subcommittee, he emphasized the necessity of taking "a really firm stand on the question of expropriation" which he described as "a disease that has been spreading in the world. . . ." [68]

Clearly the United States was able to realize its economic blockade of Chile in large part because international financial agencies are still to a large degree influenced by policy decisions in Washington. It is sufficient for a decision to be reached by the U.S. executive in order that the major lending institutions begin to fashion their policies and lending criteria accordingly. Earlier we noted the close correspondence between U.S. corporate interests and U.S. government policy and the common purposes and strategies pursued. This web of relations is now extended to include the major "international" institutions which strongly influence the international credit rating of a country. A recent study of the U.S. role in the multilateral development banks, prepared for the House Foreign Affairs Committee, has elaborated on the nature of U.S. leverage within the banks:

Although unable to quantify the extent of U.S. influence on the shaping of loan proposals and general policies in the banks, executive branch officials stress their view that there is in fact a "substantial" measure of U.S. influence, and offer specific examples illustrating the extent to which the banks have been willing to make changes in proposals upon the recommendation of the U.S. Executive Directors. In discussing the U.S. influence within the banks, Treasury officials note that while the United States is not the majority stockholder in any of the banks, it is the major stockholder in the World Bank Group and in the IDB, and one of the major stockholders in the ADB [Asian Development Bank]. The analogy suggested is that the banks, like any corporations, have an obligation to look to the interests of their principal stockholders and cannot afford any prolonged erosion of political and economic support from these members. Although no judgement is offered as to the extent of the informal influence which the United States enjoys, its existence must be recognized. It can be assumed that this indirect influence may be felt in actions the banks do not take—loan and policy proposals not presented to the boards, for example—because of expectations of a U.S. negative reaction. . . .

While the informal and indirect nature of this process makes it difficult to assess the extent of U.S. influence in loan formulation during the preparation stage, Treasury officials emphasized that the banks generally do reshape aspects of a loan which are questioned by the United States. . . .

In most instances, strongly voiced U.S. concern about an aspect of a loan appears to be sufficient to bring about a re-examination of the policy in question. Using the analogy of "losing the battle to win the war," the United States may approve a loan about which it has voiced criticisms if the loan is generally acceptable in other respects, anticipating that U.S. influence is great enough to bring pressure on the bank not to continue that policy without sufficient justification.[69]

The combined and mutually reinforcing efforts of U.S. corporations and government agencies and international banks sharply diminished the marketing, trade, investment, and credit opportunities of Chile throughout the world. No single aspect of the problem can be adequately considered in measuring the impact of the economic blockade. Only by examining the continuous process of escalating pressures in all their manifestations can we adequately appreciate the full political consequences of the U.S.-initiated and -directed efforts to overthrow the Allende government. The interlocking of business, government, and international banking that was discussed above suggests that an international power bloc has emerged whose scope of activity includes the world market and which influences a substantial area of the world's trade and credit.

Within the foreign policy machinery the formulation and

direction of foreign economic policy was largely in the hands of Treasury, the agency most closely associated with the private corporate world. While there was a consensus among all agencies in their negative evaluation of the social nature of the Allende government, there were substantial differences at different times over the adoption of specific policy measures. The National Security Council served as a sounding board and mediating body for these conflicting views, modifying and adapting them to the overall perspectives.

The Copper Conflict and the Embargo

The U.S.-based multinational corporation has been in a strategic position in the Chilean economy for over half a century. Chilean dependence and the concomitant decapitalization of the economy have been sources of economic backwardness and vulnerability. Both features of the Chilean economy have provided the multinational corporations with political and economic levers with which to limit Chile's efforts at autonomous economic development, blocking imports necessary for copper production as well as exports into foreign markets.

The legacy of Frei's "Chileanization" of the copper program was appalling: enormous foreign debts, stagnant production, and huge repatriated profit margins. The efforts of the Allende government to offset these losses and redress the balance between the national and the multinational corporations through nationalization and compensation based on a retroactive excess profits tax served as the ideological pretext for the U.S. credit and financial restrictions as well as triggering the embargo by the multinationals.

Copper policy was critical to any effort aimed at rapid and sustained national development, socialist or not. It can also be safely stated that while U.S.-owned copper was the major obstacle to autonomous development, in moving on the copper industry, the Allende government crystalized U.S. opposition, uniting the efforts of government, banks, and corporations.

The Chilean economy's historic dependence on copper has not lessened with time. It continues to account for 60 to 70 percent of total exports and approximately 80 percent of total export earnings. In 1970, U.S. corporate holdings in the copper sector accounted for 80 percent of Chile's copper production. The contribution of the copper industry to the overall development of the Chilean economy has been severely limited by three key factors: the vertically integrated "enclave" nature of the industry, with refining and fabricating plants located abroad; the use of capital-intensive technology, thus minimizing the absorption of labor; and the continued emphasis on the remittance, rather than the reinvestment, of profits.

During the first quarter of the twentieth century, the Chilean copper industry was transformed by the intrusion of a small number of large foreign (especially U.S.) corporations, which eliminated the small producer and proceeded to "organize technology and capital for the purpose of working low-grade deposits by large-scale capital-intensive methods, for the growing mass market." [70] In the following two decades, the U.S. copper companies consolidated their control over the industry, which, since 1943, has been in a state of relative stagnation. Between 1943 and 1966, output from the U.S-owned mines increased at a trend rate of less than 0.5 percent annually. For the same approximate period (1946–1966), Chile's share of the world primary copper market declined steadily from 19.6 percent to 12.7 percent.[71]

Attempts by Chilean governments, in response to nationalist pressures, to institute controls over the copper industry in the 1950s were largely unsuccessful. Increasing demands for the nationalization of the copper industry became so widespread during the 1960s, however, that the Frei administration informed the copper companies that its proposed Chileanization policy was the only alternative to more drastic action.[72] Anaconda and Kennecott agreed in 1964 to undertake their first large-scale expansion program since the initial penetration into the industry, partly for reasons of political necessity, and partly because the expansion of productive capacity at the time coincided with the overall global strategies of both U.S. multinational corporations. Furthermore, the Chilean government's proposed new twenty year tax agreement gave the companies "some reason to believe that those tax elements which were favorable to them would persist long enough for them to make rational long-term decisions." [73]

But Chileanization had no more success than previous attempts to make the U.S. copper interests responsive to the overall needs of the Chilean economy.

The main aim of "Chileanization" was to increase benefits to Chile by increasing production. The copper companies were to double output by 1972 in return for decreased taxation and other advantages, including new investment capital provided by Chilean stock purchases of 25% to 51% of the various mines, government loans, and government guaranteed loans negotiated with the Export-Import Bank and other U.S. financial institutions. Incredible as it may seem, a $579 million new investment of borrowed capital between 1966 and 1970 failed to increase production significantly. The copper corporations accumulated $632 million in debts without investing any of their own capital. Their profits, on the other hand, increased substantially due to the "Chileanization" program and rising copper prices.[74]

As the figures in Table 2 show, copper production in the *Gran Mineria* stagnated between 1966 and 1970, despite the large-scale loans contracted by the copper companies and guaranteed by the Chilean government.

A detailed study of the Chileanization program concluded

Table 2
Chile: Copper Production 1966–1970 [75]
(thousands of metric tons)

	1966	1967	1968	1969	1970
Large-scale mining operations	536	520	540	541	571

with the statement that "at every point in the negotiations . . . the foreign companies were favored." The negotiations involving Kennecott's El Teniente mine, the world's largest underground copper mine, were a case in point. "The terms under which El Teniente was partially nationalized were so generous that Kennecott ended the process of negotiation with a higher benefit-cost ratio than either of the other two foreign companies and Chile was left with practically no net benefits at all." [76] Between 1965 and 1971, the profits for Anaconda and Kennecott amounted to $426 million and $198 million, respectively.[77]

In December 1970, the Allende government introduced a constitutional amendment into the Chilean congress to nationalize the U.S.-owned copper mines. The proposed formula for compensation payments to the copper companies included deductions for capital remittances abroad, excess profits, and mine depletion. Between 1915 and 1968, Anaconda and Kennecott combined net profits and depreciation allowances from Chile totaled $2,011 million. Of this amount, only $378 million was reinvested in the industry.[78] If we consider only the period 1953 to 1968, the extent of decapitalization of the Chilean economy by the U.S. copper companies is not diminished. U.S. mining and smelting operations (approximately 90 percent copper), earned profits of $1,036 million over this fifteen year period, but reinvestments and new investments totaled a meager $71 million.[79] The extent of exploitation may be more clearly observed if we locate the Anaconda and Kennecott profits from their Chilean subsidiaries within a comparative context. The contrasts are striking. First, since 1915 "the average dollar of revenue from their Chilean operations consistently yielded a greater surplus than that of their domestic operations, except for a few years in the early 1950s." [80] Second, and more decisive, are the results obtained from a comparison of the "worldwide profitability" levels of Anaconda and Kennecott with the rate of return on their Chilean investments. Between 1955 and 1970, Anaconda showed an annual rate of return on its entire global investments of 7.18 percent, but only 3.49 percent if Chile is excluded. The rate of return on its Chilean operations alone was 20.18 percent. Kennecott's global rate of return during this period was 11.63 percent, and 10 percent excluding Chile. The figure for its Chilean operations was an astounding 34.84 percent. [81]

The U.S. government reaction to the Chilean formula for compensation was swift and pointed. Chile was given clear warning that the implementation of this formula would seriously affect U.S.-Chilean relations at the government to government level. [82] Undeterred, the Chilean congress unanimously passed the constitutional amendment in July 1971, and provided for compensation to be fixed by the controller general within ninety days.

During the last two years of the Frei government, the world price for copper exceeded any other year of the 1960s by at least 10 cents a pound. In 1969, copper sold for 66.56 cents a pound on the world market. In 1970, there was a slight decrease to 64.20 cents a pound. However, during the first two years of the Allende government, the international market price of copper declined steeply, to 49.27 cents a pound in 1971 and to 48.20 cents a pound in 1972. A reversion back to 66 cents a pound was forecast for 1973. The Chilean government mining agency, CODELCO, has estimated that for every one cent decline in the world price of copper, the copper exporting country loses some $15 million each year. If we compare the last two years of the Frei period with the three years of the Allende government (including the projected 1973 figure), we find that the average yearly price for copper on the international market was 65.38 cents a pound for 1969–1970 as compared to 54.49 cents a pound during 1971–1973. On the basis of the CODELCO estimate above, if the average yearly price for copper from 1969 to 1973 was 65.38 cents a pound, then the Allende government would have received an extra $490 million.[83]

The Anaconda Company and the Kennecott Copper Corporation reacted strongly to the Chilean controller general's decision of October 1971 that no compensation should be paid to them for their nationalized mines. Kennecott President Frank R. Milliken asserted his corporation's "determination to obtain prompt, adequate and effective compensation for its 49 percent interest in its El Teniente mine." According to the corporation the expropriation of the mine "contravene[d] accepted principles of international law."[84] Anaconda Vice-Chairman William E. Quigley declared that his company "intend[ed] to follow any legal recourse and defend itself in every way against this arbitrary indemnification by the Chilean government."[85]

In September 1972, Kennecott decided to cease further legal proceedings in Chile in support of its compensation claims, following the refusal of the Chilean Special Copper Tribunal to review the original decision. Milliken stated that Kennecott would "pursue in other nations its remedies for the confiscated assets."[86] Speculation that the corporation might attempt to embargo Chile's copper exports was reinforced by a company letter sent to all importers of Chilean copper claiming "continued rights to El Teniente copper" and informing them of the company's intention to "take all such action as may be considered necessary in order to protect our rights, including rights with regard to such copper and/or other metals or products and with regard to their proceeds."[87] Anaconda, meanwhile, continued to seek redress through the Chilean legal process, but its attention was also turned to "the possibility of additional actions in jurisdictions outside Chile." [88] For a country almost totally dependent on copper revenues (which had dropped by $200 million in 1971 as a result of declining world market prices) for its foreign exchange, the entire economy was threatened by the serious consequences of a successful or partially successful embargo.

Kennecott's strategy was subsequently defined by its General Counsel and Secretary, Pierce N. McCreary, as one of "seiz[ing] El Teniente copper wherever we find it," essentially through international legal actions designed to block payments to the Chilean Copper Corporation (CODELCO). In France, for example, a court injunction against payment of a Chilean copper shipment was only rescinded on the understanding that Chile "set aside an equal amount [in escrow] so that it can be paid to Kennecott in the case that [Chile] is found to owe money to the company." [89] A Kennecott-requested embargo on a $12.5 million shipment to West Germany, Chile's biggest copper customer, remained in effect for some time. Legal actions aimed at attaching payments for Chilean copper shipments to Britain, Sweden, Italy, Holland, the Netherlands, and other European countries were less successful, but not without impact.[90] The decision of the U.S. copper companies to utilize potential pressure points in Western Europe was necessitated by the overall direction of Chilean copper exports. In 1971, approximately 66 percent of Chile's total copper exports went to six Western European countries (Belgium, France, West Germany, Italy, Sweden, United Kingdom), while the U.S. market absorbed only 8.5 percent.[91] "Psychologically," observed a U.S. copper trader, "[Kennecott's strategy] has a very nerve-wracking effect on anybody who buys Chilean copper. It makes everybody very reluctant to get into contracts using Chilean material because they're afraid of litigation." [92] Sources within the U.S.

copper industry confirmed the development of such a trend among buyers of Chilean copper. A further consequence of Kennecott's global campaign was the suspension of loans previously negotiated by Chile with Canadian and Dutch banks.[93]

During the period of the embargo there was "a great deal of interaction" between Kennecott executives and U.S. government officials, especially within the National Security Council.[94] The other two key policy-making bodies, State and Treasury, were also in regular communication with Kennecott: "Some of the people in the international section in Treasury kept very close contact with them, and related closely to the State Department in that respect." [95] Given the close correspondence of purpose and policy, U.S. government denials of complicity in the Kennecott actions appear suspect, especially if one takes account of the cordial relations and excellent communications with the copper corporation during the course of the embargo policy. In a speech to the General Assembly of the United Nations in December 1972, Allende described in great detail the national and international politicoeconomic aggressions directed against his government by such multinational U.S. corporations as Kennecott and ITT. While refraining from any direct condemnation of the U.S. government itself, he implied that these aggressions could not be separated from a specific context, a context created and fueled by the actions of U.S. policy-makers.[96] These actions manifested themselves most visibly in the policies of the U.S. government regarding credits and loans to Chile.

The Kennecott embargo strategy occurred at a time of intense social and political struggles inside Chile. The organized opposition, with political support from the U.S. government, was attempting to create economic chaos in order to undermine the Allende government and encourage a civilian-military coup. A source close to the copper companies was led to remark that "Kennecott's legal harassment could be simply part of a bigger drive to bring down President Allende's avowedly Marxist government." [97]

With the refusal of the Chilean Special Copper Tribunal to reconsider the "no compensation" decision, and the inability of both Kennecott and Anaconda to force the Chilean government to change its position,[98] the copper companies moved to request reimbursement for their losses from the Overseas Private Investment Corporation (OPIC).

OPIC was established by the Foreign Assistance Act of 1969 as a successor to AID's investment guarantee program for U.S. corporations operating in developing countries. Its purpose was to insure U.S. investment capital "against losses from certain specific political risks" including "loss of investment due to expropriation, nationalization, or confiscation by the foreign government." [99] One observer accurately perceived that this decision to give increasing support to the global expansion of the U.S. multinational corporation could be expected to give the latter "a sense of partnership with the government," and hence, a belief in its backing in conflicts with foreign governments.[100] During recent congressional hearings on the future of OPIC, Senator Church summed up the impact of OPIC's activities on U.S. government policy: ". . . once the Government assumes the insurance of the company, the company's interest and that of the Government become identical, and the company can fall back on the Government or threaten to fall back on the U.S. Government whenever it deals with a foreign government. . . ." [101]

U.S. government policy, however, is not based on a simple "identity of interest" whereby it indiscriminately comes to the support of any threatened U.S. economic interest. OPIC policies are formulated on the basis of long-term political and economic considerations, rather than as a reflection of particular economic interests. In the case of Chile, the U.S.

government differentiated between individual corporate interests and the requirements of aggregate corporate interests. OPIC did not hesitate to intervene in compensation negotiations between the Allende government and particular U.S. corporations after both parties had reached agreement on payments. In one instance, according to an OPIC memorandum, a U.S. investor agreed to accept a Chilean government compensation offer only to be informed by OPIC that it would not give its consent to such an agreement.[102] OPIC also refused to countenance another offer of less than book value for an insured U.S. property "because of the implications of the negotiations on impending copper nationalization legislation." [103]

The private embargo initiated by the copper corporations complemented the economic pressure generated by U.S. government officials. The close ties between corporation and government reflected the common purposes pursued within different spheres of competence. Through corporate contacts in markets and political ties with U.S. officials the copper embargo became one more ingredient incorporated in the formula to overthrow the Allende government.

The Politics of the Foreign Debt

The foreign debt was like an albatross around the neck of the Allende government. Pressured to make payments, denied new loans, eager for financial assistance yet fearful of losing its credit status, the Allende government never publicly entertained the possibility of repudiating its foreign debts. Unlike the case with the credit, financial, and trade squeeze, which denied new economic resources to the government, the debt squeeze sought to extract financial resources from Chile. By demanding payments on schedule, U.S. policy-makers had a "no loss" strategy in mind: if Chile paid up it would have to divert scarce funds from popular programs and development projects, thus generating political opposition; if Chile did not pay, its international credit rating would decline, new loans from non-U.S. sources would not be forthcoming, and loss of financing of imports would cause an economic decline generating political discontent. Chilean perceptions of the U.S. bargaining position were essentially erroneous: there was no discrete set of issues that could have been negotiated and settled, least of all while U.S.-supported opposition groups in Chile were active and gaining strength. The prolonged and fruitless negotiations ostensibly over the issue of copper compensation were a ploy to which U.S. policy-makers resorted in order to conceal their more fundamental opposition to the political-economic system which was proposed in Chile. In a word, conflict over debt payments allowed the United States to embarrass the Chilean government by publicizing its shaky financial structure in a highly visible manner within an international forum, apply pressure on scarce economic resources, and exacerbate divisions within the Allende coalition.

There were high Chilean officials who eagerly sought an accommodation with the United States, believed it was possible, and were willing to limit socioeconomic changes in order to obtain it; and there were those who were less sanguine but who were unable to influence the government's course. The end result was that the U.S. position on the debt, of negotiation and no-settlement, allowed the United States to keep the pressure on without appearing to do so.

In November 1971, Allende announced that Chile would ask her foreign creditors in Western Europe and the United States to renegotiate the schedule of payments on debts accumulated, in large part by the Alessandri and Frei governments. More than half of the approximately $3.83 billion public and private debt as of December 1970 was owed to U.S. government agencies and U.S. private lenders.[104] The "Paris Club" negotiations were, not surprisingly, "complicated" by the copper issue. "It was bound to come up," observed one U.S. official.[105] In an abrupt departure from traditional practice, the position of leadership of the U.S. delegation at the Paris talks was transferred from the State Department to the Treasury Department. It was felt that Treasury would be more likely to "keep Chile's feet to the fire" over the copper expropriations.[106] Despite opposition on the part of Chile's Western European creditors to any discussion on this issue, the U.S. government was insistent that "progress in one field is tied to progress in the other." [107]

Previous attempts to reach agreement on the renegotiation of Chile's external debt failed, in part, because of Chile's refusal to accept an International Monetary Fund standby agreement as a requirement for renegotiation:

> Chile has opposed such an agreement on the grounds that it means sacrificing autonomy in internal economic policy. Such an agreement would certainly lay down norms concerning wages and prices policy, fiscal and monetary policy, and trade and exchange policy. And this would almost certainly mean an end to the present domestic expansion in Chile, a curbing of government expenditure and credit, and an insistence upon movement toward trade liberalization and devaluation. The political implications of such policies, enforced from the outside, would be extremely embarrassing for the administration.[108]

In April 1972, an agreement in principle to renegotiate Chile's debt schedule on a bilateral basis with each creditor nation was concluded. In return, Chile accepted an ambiguous compromise statement of "just compensation for all nationalizations, in conformity with Chilean and international law." [109] The creditor nations agreed to reschedule 70 percent of the interest and principal payments falling due from November 1971 through December 1972, rejecting a Chilean request for an extension until December 1974. Almost three-quarters of the $97 million eligible for rescheduling was owed to the U.S. government, which proceeded to make "just compensation" for nationalized U.S. assets a precondition for bilateral U.S.-Chilean negotiations.[110] "At that time," recalled a high-ranking Treasury official, "we brought out our concerns on [the Kennecott and Anaconda nationalizations] as being particularly germane to the whole question of creditworthiness and the rescheduling of debts." [111]

Chile was able to successfully conclude debt agreements with its Western European creditors without accepting an IMF standby loan as demanded by the United States. However, Chile was unable to moderate the rigid U.S. position on renegotiation, and no bilateral agreement was signed.

Discussions between U.S. and Chilean officials on the debt problem were resumed in late 1972, at a time of intense social and political struggle in Chile. There was no appreciable change in the U.S. position. "Washington has tied the proposed rescheduling," wrote *Business Week*, "to a settlement on expropriated U.S. properties." [112] That the Chileans were increasingly concerned to resolve this critical problem was not in doubt. Even the CIA, which was now represented on the U.S. delegation, agreed on this point:

It was our judgment that the [Chileans] were interested in working out some kind of modus vivendi without, however, retreating substantially from their position.[113]

CIA representation on the negotiating team, occurring at a time of active CIA involvement in the promotion of antigovernment demonstrations in Chile, reflected the U.S. decision to accelerate pressures on the Allende government to bring about its downfall.

In February 1973, Allende expressed his willingness to submit the copper dispute to an international commission for resolution, pursuant to a 1914 bilateral treaty between the United States and Chile (Brian Treaty) for the peaceful settlement of disputes. The Economist Intelligence Unit called the proposal "an indication of how the United States is increasingly linking the question of the renegotiation of Chile's foreign debt and renewed credit facilities to the question of just and swift compensation for the expropriated American copper companies." [114] The U.S. refusal to compromise and its rejection of the international tribunal was based on a policy of permanent confrontation. To compromise with Chile and reach an agreement would have weakened the internal opposition. In these circumstances, it is not surprising that a new round of bilateral talks in March 1973 ended abruptly "without any shred of hope that the dialogue will be continued in a friendly fashion." [115] Chilean policy-makers, nonetheless, continued in their efforts to devise a satisfactory compromise based on the assumption that the U.S. position was still based on the idea that "Chile has got to recognize the connection between copper and debt rescheduling as related subjects." [116] In fact the U.S. government's posture, however, had hardened beyond compromise.

6

The United States
and Militarism in Chile

From Congressional testimony of high military and civilian authorities it is clear that the U.S. military possessed extensive contacts among high Chilean officials, and were aware that their relationships were amenable to political influence and manipulation. U.S. military officials were convinced that restraint should be thrown to the wind and that the United States should do everything in its power to stop and reverse the socialization of Chile. There are some indications that a pre-election coup was in the making but that plans went awry. Not able to prevent Allende from coming to power, U.S. policy-makers combined a policy of economic pressures against the Allende government with selective aid directed toward the military. U.S. policy sought and succeeded in disaggregating the Chilean state, essentially establishing links with the military which in turn captured the state, purged all dissidents, and pursued a development policy within the market framework embraced by the Nixon administration.

Between 1950 and 1969, U.S. military assistance to Latin America, in the form of equipment, training, and services, totaled $1.357 billion.[1] In addition, there were visible examples of direct and indirect U.S. military intervention (Guatemala, 1954; Cuba, 1961; Dominican Republic, 1965), in support of U.S. economic interests threatened by the policies of moderate and radical nationalist political groupings. However, beginning in the early 1960s, a transformation in U.S. defense policy regarding the hemisphere began to take place. The emphasis shifted from a concern over the possibilities of external military intervention by a nonhemispheric power to a concern over the threat to the political and economic status quo represented by internal insurgency, particularly guerrilla movements. "The free world's security," declared President Kennedy, "can be endangered not only by a nuclear attack but also by being slowly nibbled away at the periphery, regardless of our strategic power, by forces of subversion, infiltration, intimidation, indirect or non-overt aggression, internal revolution, lunatic blackmail, guerrilla warfare or a series of limited wars." [2] In 1965, the director of the Military Assistance Program during the Johnson administration, General Robert Wood, asserted that:

> . . . the primary purpose of the proposed fiscal year 1965 Military Assistance Program for Latin America is to counter the threat to the entire area by providing equipment and training which will bolster the internal security capabilities of the recipient countries.[3]

Nonetheless, the Kennedy and Johnson administrations engaged in both covert and overt military activities in Latin America, and the Nixon policy of low profile or, more accurately, indirection, was essentially rooted in the conviction that direct military intervention would have a negative impact on U.S. political and economic interests in the hemisphere given the present conjuncture of events. However, wariness over the consequences of military intervention in a period of rising economic nationalism was accompanied by a policy which stressed "a very close relationship between the prospects for achieving social and economic reform and development goals and a necessary level of internal security and stability." [4] In March 1970, Secretary of Defense Melvin Laird described this policy of consolidating and improving the counterinsurgency capabilities of U.S.-oriented regimes in the area in detail.

The basic policy of decreasing direct U.S. military involvement cannot be successful unless we provide our friends and allies, whether through grant aid or credit sales, with the material assistance necessary to insure the most effective possible contribution by the manpower they are willing and able to commit to their own and the common defense. Many of them simply do not command the resources or technical capabilities to assume greater responsibility for their own defense without such assistance. The challenging objectives of our new policy can, therefore, be best achieved when each partner does its share and contributes what it best can to the common effort. In the majority of cases, this means indigenous manpower organized into properly equipped and well-trained armed forces with the help of material, training, technology and specialized skills furnished by the United States through the Military Assistance Program or as Foreign Military Sales.[5]

The report in early 1970 of a special congressional study mission to assess the military assistance training program in Latin America was more direct.

In conclusion, the study mission wishes to point out that the majority of issues which must be addressed about MAP training are political and economic in nature, rather than strictly military. This emphasis reflects our strong convictions that military assistance programs are primarily an instrument of American foreign policy and only secondarily of defense policy.[6]

A staff memorandum on U.S. military assistance and U.S. AID public safety programs in Guatemala and the Dominican Republic, prepared later that year for the Senate Foreign

Relations Committee, suggested that this indeed was the basis for U.S. military aid to the hemisphere. It was highly critical of the "political price" involved in maintaining these programs in authoritarian and clientele Latin countries. The study concluded its analysis of the Dominican Republic program with the observation that "when all of the rhetoric is stripped away, the basic justification for the military assistance program is that the program provides an excuse for the MAAG [Military Assistance Advisory Group] and the MAAG keeps in touch with what the Dominican military are thinking." [7]

The U.S. response to the overthrow of the nationalist Torres government in Bolivia in August 1971 by a right-wing military coup offers an excellent example of the way in which military aid has been utilized for political and economic ends by the Nixon administration. After testifying before the House Appropriations Subcommittee in April 1972 on foreign assistance appropriations for fiscal year 1973, General George M. Seignious II, Deputy Assistant Secretary of Defense for International Security Affairs, engaged in debate with Subcommittee Chairman Otto Passman:

GENERAL SEIGNIOUS. The best example of our military grant aid material going into Latin America is Bolivia. That is where the largest program is $4.8 million. There is a President now in Bolivia that is somewhat U.S. oriented and he is faced with dissident elements both internally and externally. . . .We feel that it is in the national interest to strengthen the current regime in Bolivia to maintain internal security.

MR. PASSMAN. Our national interest or Bolivia's national interest?

GENERAL SEIGNIOUS. We feel it is in the interest of both Bolivia and the United States.

MR. PASSMAN. Make the case for the United States, if you will.

GENERAL SEIGNIOUS. We have now, in Bolivia, a country that is at least nominally oriented toward the United States. We feel that for the small expenditure of support in the way of grant aid that that Government can defeat or deny the extension of the insurgency.[8]

Since 1969, occasional differences and tensions over specific issues with Latin American countries under military rule have led to temporary or short-term conflicts with the United States. Nevertheless, the United States has continued to stress the importance of maintaining channels of influence and direction with the Latin American military as one of the major instruments of social control and preservation of the dominant political elites and economic ruling classes in the region. A high-level Defense Department policy-maker outlined the rationale behind U.S. military assistance policy toward Latin America:

> We are furnishing assistance in the form of military training to almost all of the countries of Latin America. It is sometimes difficult to sort out those that have elected governments from those that don't. We feel it is extremely important to maintain our relations with the people who are in positions of influence in those countries so we can help to influence the course of events in those countries.[9]

The U.S. Southern Command has a very clear conception of its political tasks in pursuit of U.S. politico-economic interests in Latin America. During questioning of General George R. Mather, U.S. Army, Commander in Chief, U.S. Southern Command, by the House Foreign Affairs Subcommittee on Inter-American Affairs, in 1970, a highly suggestive discussion occurred.

MR. FASCELL. That report that we referred to stressed the theme that your command played a very important or significant political role, and stressed the fact in describing that, that since most of the leaders in Latin America were military men that military men in SOUTHCOM could best deal with them. This was the emphasis of the political aspects of SOUTHCOM. Do you personally conceive of your command as playing any kind of a political role in South America either in that aspect or some other aspect?

MR. GROSS. Or your staff?

GENERAL MATHER. Directly; no. I want to answer that question very, very carefully, Mr. Chairman. First of all, it is a fact, I believe, that the military in Latin America play a very definite role in the political process.

MR. FASCELL. I think we could take judicial notice of that fact.

GENERAL MATHER. OK. Given that, then, I have an excellent channel to that very important element in this political process.

MR. FASCELL. Do you mean through your MIL Groups [U.S. Military Advisory Group] in these 17 countries?

GENERAL MATHER. Exactly. This can be of significant assistance in the conduct of our relations in support of our national purpose. Now, to that extent there is a political aspect to this relationship.

MR. FASCELL. Do you mean as a base of direct communication?

GENERAL MATHER. This is right.

MR. FASCELL. I mean in the political process of the local country?

GENERAL MATHER. Yes, as a means of information and communication for the use of our Ambassadors. The MIL Group contacts have, on occasion and for short periods, been the best channel open.[10]

General Mather was also questioned on the issue of U.S. government support for authoritarian military regimes in Latin America. He viewed such support as "so important to our national security that we should be prepared to, somehow or other, live with the excesses of which many of them are accused [security deletion]." He equated U.S. national security interests with the prevention of "another Cuba," which prompted Subcommittee Chairman Fascell to raise the issue of the nature of the U.S. response to a hypothetical Communist electoral victory in Chile, only a matter of weeks prior to the 1970 national election in Chile, where a coalition of leftist political forces was given a good chance of obtaining the presidency. "I don't see," Fascell declared, "how the United States could have a direct military response to that event." The exchange continued:

GENERAL MATHER. I don't either, Mr. Chairman. I just hope that it doesn't happen. As you know, our record of recovery of countries that have gone down the drain is practically nil. We haven't gotten any of them back once they have gone. This is what we have got to stop.

MR. FASCELL. What you are saying here is, that we, as a government, ought to take every action we can which would prevent such an occurrence. Particularly since we are limited in our capability to react?

GENERAL MATHER. Yes, sir.[11]

These exchanges appear to have been in keeping with the general tenor of U.S. policy regarding the upcoming Chilean election in September 1970. Since January, the U.S. navy had made applications for Chilean visas for eighty-seven officers and civilian employees. Chilean government inquiries regarding this phenomenon elicited a series of contradictory responses from the Defense Department and the Department of State. An explanation that the visas were for a goodwill navy band tour surprised Chilean officials "because there was no record that such a visit was planned [and] the ranks of the men involved made it unlikely that they were musicians." A number of the officers held academic degrees in physics, space, aeroengineering, computer science, and marine biology. Several were naval aviators qualified as destroyer and submarine commanders "and at least one took graduate studies in defense intelligence. . . ." The Chilean embassy was subsequently informed by the State Department that forty-nine of the visas were actually for U.S. personnel involved in the coming joint annual antisubmarine warfare exercises. Yet, Chile had officially decided not to participate in these exercises some months previously in order "to avoid the possibility that the presence of American warships in Chilean waters would be interpreted as a sign of United States political pressure." U.S. officials did not offer any clarification on this point. The State Department had also maintained that a further thirty-eight visas were for U.S. Antarctic personnel to travel to the U.S. installation at Palmer Base, which is supplied through the Chilean port of Punta Arenas. According to the U.S. navy, however, the normal complement of base personnel is ten men. It should be noted, in conclusion, that all the officers for whom visas were requested were classified as "unrestricted line officers," which designated them available for any type of duty.[12]

Immediately after Allende's inauguration as president, General Mather, in his capacity as head of the U.S. Southern Command, held discussions with the leaders of the Chilean armed forces. He emphasized, however, that this action "does not in any way imply a circumvention of the Ambassador nor his responsibility there, since my entire effort and that of my military group is in conjuncture with his overall responsibility." [13]

In mid-1971, against the background of an emerging aggressive foreign economic policy regarding countries expropriating U.S. economic assets, directed primarily at the Allende government, the United States decided to grant a Chilean request for $5 million in military credits as part of its "pragmatic policy." [14] Secretary of State Rogers noted that "it is quite interesting that in the case of Latin America we are still providing some military assistance to Chile, for the reasons we think it would be better not to have a complete break with them." [15] In December 1972, the U.S. government announced that a $10 million credit agreement for the Chilean military, signed in May, would be granted, notwithstanding the January 1972 policy statement on aid to governments expropriating U.S.-owned properties without prompt, adequate, and effective compensation.[16] The House Appropriations Subcommittee on Foreign Assistance, through its Chairman, Otto Passman, took a highly critical view of this military assistance to Chile during hearings on the 1974 foreign assistance appropriations. The officials being questioned were Vice-Admiral Ray Peet, Director of the Defense Security Assistance Agency and Deputy Assistant Secretary of Defense (International Security Affairs) for Security Assistance, and Curtis W. Tarr, Deputy Under-Secretary of State for Coordinating Security Assistance Programs.

MR. PASSMAN. First let us take Chile. How can you justify an aid program in Chile?

ADMIRAL PEET. From a Defense Department point of view, we consider Chile a political problem and therefore primarily a matter of state interest._____ _____.

MR. PASSMAN. Let us get back to the basics. You are talking about a Communist form of government.

ADMIRAL PEET. In Chile, yes, sir.

MR. PASSMAN. They expropriated all the American company properties, did they not? Could a country be any more Communist than Chile?

ADMIRAL PEET. I would prefer that State answer that question.

MR. PASSMAN. Could they? Do you know of any country that could be any more Communist than Chile?

MR. TARR. Mr. Chairman, I think you are right. The problem here is the orientation of the government and the hope is to _____.

MR. LONG. Buy them off.

MR. TARR. ——————————————.

MR. PASSMAN. How could they get any closer to communism than they are?

ADMIRAL PEET. They can't. However, we are maintaining influence; —————.[17]

As early as April 1970, the U.S. government had been considering the possibility of employing its waiver power under Section 4 of the Foreign Military Sales Act in order to sell jet aircraft to a number of Latin American countries, including Chile. Concern was expressed over countries finding alternative sources of supply and over "the cost to our political relations with these countries of our continued inability to supply aircraft which they consider reasonable and necessary for the modernization of their forces."[18] In May 1973, President Nixon decided to exercise the waiver authority to allow five Latin American countries, including Chile, to purchase F-5E military fighter aircraft, on the grounds that such action was "important to the national security of the United States."[19]

On September 11, 1973, a military coup overthrew the democratic socialist government of Chile. "The Chilean armed forces and carabineros," declared a military junta communiqué, "are united to initiate the historic and responsible mission to fight for the liberation of the fatherland from the Marxist yoke. . . ."[20] Former President Eduardo Frei and influential sectors of the Christian Democratic Party voiced their unqualified support for the coup. The party's governing council issued an official statement which asserted that the Allende government "was preparing to stage a violent coup . . . in order to install a Communist dictatorship. Everything indicates that the armed forces did nothing more than to respond to this immediate risk."[21] Having laid the basis for the coup it was not surprising that the United

States was unwilling to publicly protest the violent and unconstitutional overthrow of an elected government. Through its strategically placed officials, agents, and operatives active in Chile the U.S. government received advance knowledge of the coup. Yet for propaganda purposes, policy-makers decided to maintain a posture of noninvolvement: ". . . Washington at 'the highest level' decided on a hands-off policy after evaluating the information. . . . this meant that President Nixon was notified." [22] After the first day of the coup, when it became apparent that direct U.S. military intervention would not be necessary, the White House began its campaign denying any U.S. involvement in the coup.[23] The latter position was forcefully stated by Jack Kubisch, Assistant Secretary of State for Inter-American Affairs, in testimony before the House Foreign Affairs Subcommittee on Inter-American Affairs.

> I wish to state as flatly and as categorically as I possibly can that we did not have advance knowledge of the coup that took place on September 11. . . . there was no contact whatsoever by the organizers and leaders of the coup directly with us, and we did not have definite knowledge of it in advance.
>
> In a similar vein, either explicitly or implicitly, the U.S. Government has been charged with involvement or complicity in the coup. This is absolutely false. As official spokesmen of the U.S. Government have stated repeatedly, we were not involved in the coup in any way.[24]

As we have shown above, Washington did indeed play a crucial role in establishing the political and social conditions for the coup through its economic policies. Moreover, the relative lack of detailed factual information on U.S. involvement in the coup must be seen in the context of a political system where covert politics plays a vital role. The exact role of the United States in the mechanics of the execution of the military aspects of the coup can only be inferred from scanty evidence. What is clear, however, is that the divergence between public statements and covert actions has been a characteristic of U.S. policy toward the Allende government from the beginning. Kubisch's statement categorically denying U.S. complicity in the coup was followed by a refusal to deny U.S. government financing of the activities of various opposition groups to the Allende government in the precoup period. He offered to discuss the matter in closed executive session so as not "to give a misleading impression abroad. . . ." [25]

From these accounts and from the peculiar circumstances surrounding the behavior of U.S. officials one is led to the conclusion that the U.S. government played an important role in the highly organized and coordinated military operation that culminated in the overthrow of the Allende government. The U.S. Ambassador to Chile, Nathaniel Davis, returned to Washington for discussions with Secretary of State-designate Kissinger and a special "Chile group" within the National Security Council, and then rejoined the U.S. embassy staff in Santiago during the week preceding the coup. This was the same "group" which designed the general policy of opposing Allende and which perhaps had been responsible for shifting the timetable for the military coup. On the day the coup took place, four U.S. navy vessels were headed for Chile to engage in joint hemispheric maneuvers but, according to the State Department, were rerouted once news of the conflict was received.[26] Subsequently, it was determined that a number of U.S. navy officers were in Valparaiso and in contact with the Chilean naval officials who initiated the coup.

A congressional subcommittee inquiring into the events surrounding the military coup in Chile, and the activities of U.S. military personnel, with Assistant Secretary of State Kubisch does not provide much in the way of substantive information nor does it describe accurately the close ties and political perspectives of the U.S. and Chilean military officials.[27] Department of Defense officials were almost as vague:

> Our support of the Chilean military has more or less continued uninterrupted before, during and after the Allende regime . . . because we made a specific effort to maintain close relations with the Chilean military.[28]

The State Department took the same tack of admitting extensive interaction between U.S. civilian and military personnel and the Chilean military, but placed their relations within a "routine," "normal" bureaucratic setting, thus attempting to obscure possible political ties.[29]

An account of the activities of U.S. military and civilian personnel in the port city of Valparaiso prior to and during the coup suggests that these "contacts" were not limited to "routine" duties. The report, authorized by Charles E. Horman, a U.S. resident in Chile subsequently killed by the junta, quoted a retired U.S. engineer formerly stationed in the Panama Canal Zone as saying: "We came down to do a job and it's done." [30]

The Role of the CIA in the Nixon-Kissinger Policy

Throughout the Allende years there were frequent reports of CIA involvement in Chile's internal politics. These accounts were always categorically denied by U.S. officials up to and including President Nixon and his chief foreign policy advisor, Henry Kissinger. During congressional hearings held on his nomination to be secretary of state on September 17, 1973 (a matter of days following the military coup in Chile), Kissinger addressed himself to this particular point:

> The CIA had nothing to do with the coup, to the best of *my* knowledge and belief, and I only put in that qualification

in case some madman down there who without instructions, talked to somebody. I have absolutely no reason to suppose it. [Deleted].[31]

The secret testimony of William E. Colby, Director of the CIA, before the House Foreign Affairs Committee offers a striking contrast to the professed U.S. public position of noninvolvement in the internal social and political struggles in Chile leading up to the coup. The publication of large sections of Colby's testimony, initially by Tad Szulc[32] and most recently by Seymour M. Hersh,[33] partially reveals the degree to which covert subversion complemented by official lies and deceit, as well as criminal perjury,[34] were at the heart of U.S. policy to Chile.

In elaborating on the CIA's involvement it is useful to recall the institutional context within which the CIA operates and the political responsibility for its activities. As we pointed out earlier, the CIA is not an independent "invisible government" within the government undermining the policies or evading the control of responsible elected or appointed officials in the executive branch. As one U.S. official forcefully put it: "You have the straight out policy that the United States conducts covert actions on an *officially authorized basis. . . .*"[35] The CIA operations in Chile were, according to Colby, approved in advance by the Committee of Forty in Washington, the secret high-level intelligence panel which is presided over by Secretary of State Kissinger. The CIA was, and is, an arm of U.S. policy: its destructive activities are an integral part of U.S. policy efforts to undermine popular, nationalist, and democratic-socialist governments: what are described in Kissingeresque language as "antagonistic governments."

According to Colby's testimony, $500,000 was secretly authorized by the Committee of Forty in 1969 and again in 1970. The funds were allocated to influence the election; there is no clear indication of how the funds were allocated in 1969, though an unsuccessful military coup did take place. Between the election of Allende in September 1970 and his inauguration in November of the same year, Colby's testimony reveals that $350,000 had been authorized by the Committee of Forty in an unsuccessful effort to bribe members of the Chilean congress. Colby's testimony stands in sharp contradiction to previous statements before the Multinationals Subcommittee of the Senate Foreign Relations Committee by the former U.S. Ambassador to Chile, Edward Korry, and the former Secretary of State for Inter-American Affairs Charles Meyer. Meyer insisted that the U.S. "financed no candidates, no political parties before or after the September 8 or September 4 [elections] rather, and. . . ." [36] Korry was even more categorical:

> The United States did not get involved in the so-called Alessandri formula. The United States did not seek to pressure, subvert, influence, a single member of the Chilean Congress at any time in my entire four years. [37]

In his discussion of this period Colby raises a whole new series of questions regarding possible U.S. involvement in the terrorist activity which culminated in the assassination of the commander in chief of the Chilean armed forces, General Rene Schneider. According to Colby, the bribe was part of a much more complicated scheme to overturn the results of the election but the overall plan, although initially approved by the Committee of Forty, was later rejected as unworkable. Several questions arise from this testimony: at what point in its implementation, after its initial approval, was this "complicated scheme" rejected as unworkable? Was the terror-kidnap-assassination effort to overturn the results of the election rejected as unworkable, after it failed? All the evidence is not yet available, but testimony suggests that the United States may have been involved in the assassination of General Schneider.

Subsequent to Allende's inauguration and for the remainder of his term in office, the CIA, according to Colby, engaged in subversive activity ("destabilization efforts" in the CIA's lexicon), on a budget of at least $6.5 million, $1.5 million of which was used to finance anti-Allende candidates in the 1973 congressional elections. These funds were utilized to finance mass media (including *El Mercurio*, the Chilean equivalent of the *New York Times*), political parties, and others. The funds were channeled into Chile through organizations outside of Chile, with Brazil being the likeliest conduit. Brazilians who have been involved in the activities leading to the coup admit supporting employer boycotts, women's demonstrations and the training of Chilean rightwing extremists. The CIA's initial budgetary allocation was increased by $1 million in August 1973, one month before the coup, for "further political destabilization activities." It is quite likely that the truckers' strike was financed by the foreign, probably Brazilian, conduits through which the CIA operated, a point Colby refused to rule out. Nevertheless, two weeks after the coup, Assistant Secretary of State for Inter-American Affairs Jack Kubisch denied "categorically" that the U.S. government or the CIA was involved in the truckers' strike or other strikes during this period of heightened social tension.[38]

While Colby's testimony has not revealed the full extent of CIA involvement, enough has been said to safely conclude that U.S. involvement was pervasive, continuous, and inserted itself in many of the most vital areas of the Chilean political process. The following exchange between Colby and Congressman Fascell is indicative:

MR. FASCELL. Is it reasonable to assume that the Agency has penetrated all of the political parties in Chile?

MR. COLBY. I wish I could say yes. I cannot assure you all, because we get into some splinters.

MR. FASCELL. Major?

MR. COLBY. I think we have an intelligence coverage of most of them. Let's put it that way.

MR. FASCELL. Is that standard operating procedure?

MR. COLBY. It depends on the country. For a country of the importance of Chile to the United States' decision-making, we would try to get an inside picture of what is going on there.[39]

The CIA's role was designed and directed by the leading members of the executive branch of the U.S. government. The common outlook among the various agencies of the executive branch clearly reveals the nature of the U.S. political system: faced by a challenge to U.S. imperial domination, the liberals and conservatives, military and civilians, the State Department and the Pentagon, joined forces to fashion policies and measures (under the overall direction of the Committee of Forty chaired by Henry Kissinger) to destroy the "enemy": an elected government in Chile. The differences among the bureaucratic hierarchies were at best tactical; the strategic goals were the same. One official noted:

> In the period before the coup . . . there was a pretty firm view on the 40 Committee—which is Kissinger and nobody else—that the Allende government was bound to come to destruction [sic] and had to be thoroughly discredited. The State Department supported this but in a different way. . . . It wanted to stretch out any clandestine activities to permit the regime to come to a political end. The argument was between those who wanted to use force and end it quickly rather than to play it out. Henry was on the scale of the former—he was for considerable obstruction.[40]

Twenty-thousand Chileans have been killed, tens of thousands have been tortured and jailed as a direct result of Kissinger's Chilean policies. It was the height of obscenity to grant him the Nobel Peace Prize during the years in which he was the architect of the policies which would lead to the destruction of Chilean democracy and to the slaughter of tens of thousands of its citizens. No single individual has greater responsibility for the criminal events in Chile than Henry Kissinger.

Beyond the issue of personal responsibility is the larger issue of the nature of the U.S. political system and the making of its foreign policy. What is clear is not only the counterrevolutionary nature of U.S. policy, its opposition to a democratically elected socialist government intent on structural changes, but the fact that the collective interests of U.S. capitalism as represented in the executive branch are not subject to any type of democratic control. The efforts by the progressive liberal Congressman Harrington to interest Congress in the issues raised by CIA involvement were largely fruitless. The numerous State Department officials including Henry Kissinger who testified under oath that the United States was not making any efforts to interfere in Chilean internal politics have not been prosecuted for perjury. It is clear that where the interests of U.S. imperialism conflict with the institutions, rules, and norms of a bourgeois democracy it is the latter that must give way. In systemic terms, faced with a challenge to U.S. imperial hegemony, power becomes centralized and stylistic, and particularistic differences and rivalries within the several agencies and their apparatuses are submerged. A threat to the collective interests of the U.S. ruling class coalesces the political apparatus in the executive and crystalizes action. Ritualistic disavowal of covert subversive action parallels the implementation of precisely this type of activity. Congress looks the other way, in disinterest, impotence, ignorance, and/or as an accomplice. Academic apologists and the mass media prepare articles and speeches blaming the victim for the crimes which are to befall it. After the events have transpired, the goals accomplished, there may be some efforts made to "uncover the truth." The "lies of state" are uncovered, the media may report the inconvenient facts, the actors will refuse to comment, the academic apologists will be dutifully exposed, and U.S. imperialism will continue to function because the state structures and the classes they represent will continue to dominate U.S. society and require Chilean-type coups, and Kissinger-style subversion. The personalities and policies involved in the overthrow of Allende, the support of the current Chilean junta, and the Brazilian dictatorship are outgrowths of the U.S. political economy. Unless U.S. society is transformed, an imperial foreign policy is inescapable.

The United States, the Multilateral Agencies, and the Creditworthy Military Government

U.S. policy toward the Allende government was a policy of unrelenting hostility designed to make it impossible for the Allende coalition to succeed itself; to conclusively demonstrate that the Marxist government is and was a failure. The policy never changed from the day Allende was elected.[41]

. . . as of November 1971, Chile was a clear case of a country not being creditworthy as shown by the fact that Chile did suspend debt service payments. Not creditworthy, whatever that may mean.[42]

The U.S. government was "delighted with the turn of events [that] eliminated a socialist government [in Chile]" [43] and replaced it with one more consonant with U.S. policy goals in Latin America. A prominent State Department official summarized the overall U.S. position:

Our general view was, quite naturally, that this government, any non-Marxist government in Chile, in terms of immediate, concrete U.S. interests was advantageous.[44]

Chile under Allende was regarded by the United States as the primary threat to its hemispheric interests. This was indirectly alluded to by a number of policy-makers in their comments on the strengthened U.S. position in Latin America as a result of the military coup.

> U.S. policy in Latin America since the overthrow of the Allende government—I should think our position has toughened in every respect, e.g., there has been a settlement in Peru, Kissinger's meeting here and in Mexico with the Foreign Ministers.[45]

> [The coup] has been helpful from the point of view of a couple of countries which no longer have the Chilean Allende-type Marxist regime as a worse alternative. It has improved the U.S. position in every respect, notably in Peru.[46]

Although some voices were raised in the U.S. Congress mildly critical of U.S. support for the military junta (most notably that of Senator Kennedy), such criticism had "zero" impact on policy-making.[47] And, in fact, the more widespread congressional view was probably closer to that of Senator McGee, Chairman of the Senate Foreign Relations Subcommittee on Latin America, who apparently disagreed with U.S. policy "only in that it took so long to remove Allende—which is now the reason why it is all so bloody." [48]

Congressional objections to the totalitarian terror policies of the autocratic military regime produced responses from policy-makers which ranged from cynical know-nothingness ("Regarding the human rights aspects, I don't know how much of any of it is true. . . . I don't say that they are using harsh methods. . . ." [49]); to perfunctory and meaningless statements of concern ("The Department has taken into consideration the totality of U.S. policy interests in planning for U.S. assistance to Chile. Congressional interest in human rights . . . has of course been carefully borne in mind." [50]); to explicit apologies of the terror in terms of its beneficial consequences:

> Politically, when you have any coup like this, it is almost inevitable that social humanitarian problems arise. Excesses are inherent in any change of government that occurs through force and moves to a parliamentary orderly takeover. It is true that the government has carried out a policy of repression, but not a conscious, deliberate repression, and it results in (1) re-establishing of internal order; and (2) international pressure focused on the problem.[51]

Congressional personnel themselves seriously questioned their ability to exercise leverage over the White House on this matter in any case.

> [The White House] has a minimal concern with the human rights question. There is not a single individual in the Executive Branch who spends more than ten seconds worrying about that kind of issue.[52]

The executive branch was especially enthusiastic over the social character of the military coup. Repression was directed against workers, peasants, slum dwellers, those groups in society geographically and socially identified with the Allende government; this was followed by the elaboration of economic policies designed to signal a reversion to dependence on foreign investment. Together these measures gave the coup its specific social character: pro-capitalist and pro-United States. One U.S. official addressed himself to this point:

> Economically, they immediately proceeded to rescind, reverse the direction toward nationalization of private enterprise, an immediate indication on their part that they were going to compensate for what was nationalized. The main problem is their inability, not reluctance, to pay. They opened up the economy internally and externally to private capital. It

is true that they are still struggling and not getting a hold on the problems that have built up. Still, you have a terribly messed up economy which can't be turned around overnight.[53]

The military regime discarded completely the Allende government's nationalist foreign policy, became unconditional supporters of U.S. policies and business interests, and outlined a new development strategy designed to encourage foreign capital investment. These political measures re-established Chile's international creditworthiness. The junta severed diplomatic and economic relations with Cuba, gave notice of its intention to play a less dynamic role within the Andean Pact and in regard to such issues as the 200-mile fishing rights dispute, and was the most energetic defender of the United States at the foreign ministers' meeting in Mexico in February 1974. The vast majority of foreign and domestic enterprises intervened in or nationalized during the preceding three years would, it was announced, be returned to their original owners, and the junta agreed in principle to paying compensation to the U.S. copper companies.[54] Understandably, "the overall U.S. response to the policies of the military government have been very supportive . . . if you compare our stance now with say July 1973, it's almost a 180 degree turn." [55]

In the light of these measures taken by the junta, the U.S. government, the foreign private banking community, and the multilateral financial institutions reversed their policies and offered support to the badly battered Chilean economy.

The U.S. decision (September 25) to maintain diplomatic relations with the new military junta was the result of a secret conference between Ambassador Davis and Secretary of State Kissinger, held "reportedly to discuss means by which the United States can come speedily to the aid of the junta." [56] The U.S. government was "the first to make financial overtures" in the form of a Department of Agriculture $24 million credit for the purchase of "desperately needed wheat," followed by a further $28 million credit for the purchase of corn.[57] The *Journal of Commerce* called the three year wheat credit "extraordinary" in view of prior U.S. policy which had been based on Chile's supposed lack of creditworthiness.[58] Senator Kennedy noted that the wheat credit "[was] eight times the total commodity credit offered to Chile in the past three years when a democratically elected government was in power."[59] Prior to the coup, a Chilean agricultural trade delegation had attempted, unsuccessfully, to obtain emergency wheat credits from the U.S. government. Pedro Bosch, the purchasing agent for the delegation, remarked at the time that such credits were fundamentally dependent on a "political decision of the White House. . . ."[60]

In December 1973, the U.S. government agreed to renegotiate part of Chile's foreign debt to U.S. government agencies after the military junta "made statements about compensation [for the expropriated U.S. copper companies] that indicated they were serious about it." Under the terms of the renegotiation, Chile agreed to pay $60 million over a four year period and a further $64 million over a six year period beginning in January 1975.[61] The fact remains, however, that the Nixon administration "made an about-face."[62] The agreement was secured prior to a compensation settlement with the copper companies. Previously, U.S. policy-makers, both in the Paris Club meetings and in bilateral U.S.-Chilean discussions, had made this a precondition for any renegotiation of Chile's foreign debt. An official in the executive branch of the U.S. government involved with international economic policy agreed that the U.S. position had changed.

It is fair to say that we took a different view on terms and conditions of rescheduling with the new regime. For example, we were trying in the previous debt rescheduling negotiations with the Allende regime to use that as leverage for some progress on the investment compensation issue. The new regime said, "Yes, that's no problem, we will start negotiations tomorrow to eliminate unjust things Allende government attempted to impose." [63]

One consequence of this changed U.S. position was the decision of the Export-Import Bank to reconsider its lending policy toward Chile.[64]

The anticommunist military dictatorship also received immediate aid and encouragement from the international banking community. *Business Latin America* observed, somewhat caustically, that the major justification for Chile's "three years of almost total ostracism" by the international banking community continued to exist despite the change in government.

> The bankers' quick response to the junta's plea for "a little Marshall Plan" is something of a mystery. For one thing, the military cried out that the economy was on the brink of bankruptcy when it took over. Moreover, the renegotiation of Chile's onerous *past* foreign debt, now estimated to total $4 billion, has yet to take place. Until that problem is solved, the question of Chile's creditworthiness, which was attacked by the international banking community during the Allende regime, remains unanswered.[65]

The availability of loans from U.S. private banks to Chile increased almost immediately after the junta took power. Whereas lines of short-term commercial credit had hovered at around $300 million during the Alessandri-Frei years, by the end of 1971 they had declined to $25-$30 million. Since the coup, the predictions that "these lines of credit could . . . eventually climb to the levels they had reached before Allende took office" [66] have been amply confirmed in practice. During the first month of junta rule, approximately

$200 million in new lines of credit was extended, primarily by U.S. banks.[67] These credits were short-term commercial credits enabling the government to meet its immediate obligations and to purchase products essential to the day-to-day functioning of the Chilean economy.

The international agencies took up the slack in the area of credits for long-term development projects. Missions from the World Bank, the International Monetary Fund, the Inter-American Development Bank, and the Inter-American Committee for the Alliance for Progress (CIAP) "flocked to Santiago" and, according to the Central Bank president General Eduardo Cano, appeared "well-disposed" toward the junta.[68] The Inter-American Development Bank actually approved an $8.5 million loan to CORFO (the Chilean Development Corporation) for a rural electrification program before its mission study was completed. The World Bank granted a $13.0 million technical assistance credit to the junta and agreed to provide CORFO with $5.25 million for preinvestment studies in mining, metallurgy, manufacturing, transportation, etc. The International Monetary Fund approved a $95 million standby agreement in February 1974, which played a decisive role in pushing the Paris Club countries to agree to renegotiate Chile's over $900 million foreign debt in May.[69]

During its first six months, the Chilean military dictatorship has benefited from the new financial largesse shown toward Chile by the international capitalist world: approximately $470 million in loans and credits from the United States, Brazil, Argentina, and the international institutions (see Table 3); $100 million in short-term credits from a U.S. banking consortium; and scheduled credits of $10 million each from the Banco de Colombia and a Swiss foreign trade financial commission.[70]

The U.S. government and U.S. private creditors have been active in other ways. Chile has received an $11 million

Table 3
Foreign Credits Granted Chile, September 1973–March 1974

	Totals in millions of U.S. $
Government to government loans	146.0
From United States	49.0
Corn purchases	28.0
Wheat purchases	21.0
From Brazil	62.0
Free disposability	50.0
Sugar purchases	12.0
From Argentina	35.0
Reproductive cattle	20.0
Agricultural machinery	15.0
International institutions	322.8
International Monetary Fund	
(contingent credit—standby)	95.0
World Bank	18.25
Preinvestment studies	5.25
Technical assistance to the public sector	13.0
Inter-American Development Bank	201.0
Loan announced by IDB's president in USA*	30.0
For agriculture	25.0
For electrification	70.0
For irrigation works	45.7
For reforestation	15.0
For CORFO projects	10.0
For social development	6.0
Andean Development Corporation	8.55
For aircraft leasing	8.55
Total of foreign loans	468.8

* No details are given on loan destination.

military credit from the U.S. government, and for fiscal year 1975 the Nixon administration has submitted to Congress a $21.3 million military aid package for Chile. Proposed U.S. economic assistance for Chile in 1975 totals $63.7 million.[71] The U.S. Export-Import Bank has resumed its guarantee and insurance programs for Chile, and shortly after the coup a U.S. banking consortium refinanced $124 million of an undischarged debt maintained by Chile with the consortium since 1971.[72] In June the First National City Bank of New York purchased more than half (approximately $11.2 million) of ten billion escudos' worth of treasury notes issued at the beginning of the month by the Chilean government.[73] Finally, during the latter half of 1974 "substantial amounts of wheat and other foodstuffs are expected to be made available" under the U.S. government's PL 480 Title 1 program.[74]

In collaboration with the other members of the Paris Club, the U.S. government also played a key role in the decision taken by Chile's international creditors in late March to reschedule 80 percent of the country's $750 million debt over a seven year period beginning in 1977. *Business Latin America* called the agreement "surprisingly generous," while *Latin America Economic Report* declared it to be "an important psychological step in clearing the way for new credits to Chile." [75] A British financier responded to the agreement as follows: "Bankers are like sheep; they all feel a lot better now that the Club has formally said okay." [76] Within less than a month, credits totaling $140 million from Brazil, France, Finland, Belgium, and East Germany had been earmarked for Enami, the state mining corporation.[77] Despite problems over the human rights issue with some Paris Club creditors during the follow-up bilateral negotiations on the foreign debt (e.g., England), foreign investors seemed anxious and eager to support the economic rehabilitation of a dependent capitalist Chile. "International lenders," one source observed, "continue to fall over each other in their haste to provide the junta with ready cash." [78]

The international banks have made substantial grants to the junta despite the lack of evidence suggesting an upturn in the economy in the foreseeable future. It is interesting to note in this respect that of the $201 million approved by the Inter-American Development Bank up to March 1974, $171 million was done so on extremely generous terms as far as Chile was concerned: a thirty year repayment period, with seven years' grace, at two percent interest per annum. In May the IDB approved two further loans (for electric power and agricultural development), totaling $97.3 million.[79] The management and staff of the Inter-American Development Bank "were very eager" [80] to establish new lines of credit with the Chilean junta, at least as much for political as for economic reasons. An example of the IDB bureaucracy's scant concern with developmental criteria was the $22 million agricultural credit "rammed through" [81] in time for the annual meeting of the IDB in Santiago in April 1974.

> The clearest change [within the multilateral agencies] was in the Inter-American Development Bank. They worked very fast, in part because of the pressure of the General Assembly of the IDB meeting in Santiago in April 1974. There was an agricultural loan program given at the end of March 1974 for $22 million. It was processed in one month which was incredible. Usually such projects take six months or more. Maybe both internal pressures and the Santiago meeting [contributed to this decision]. The situation in the agricultural sector in Chile was bad enough as to justify the need. However, it was not clear how well organized the agricultural sector was to absorb $20 million so fast. A lot of problems in [the area of] technical assistance to agrarian reform, so difficult to think that they could manage to absorb $20 million so fast.[82]

At one point, the West German government tried unsuccessfully to pressure the IDB to moderate its economic assistance program to the military dictatorship to show its concern over the internal political situation in Chile.

> In December 1973, the IDB had planned to sell some bonds in the German capital market. The Germans told them

that if they were going to go ahead with large programs to Chile the German government was not ready to allow the IDB to sell those bonds in the German market. This held up operations from the IDB to Chile for a time. The Germans changed their position in March 1974 or the IDB found alternative sources of funds.[83]

Some U.S. policy-makers have grudgingly admitted that "[the junta's] economic policies have been only partially successful," [84] but have sought to rationalize the disappointing economic performance by arguing that, in the short-term at least, the question of political stability and internal security must take precedence. Unlike the World Bank, which has also criticized the junta's economic policies, the U.S. government is making no effort to scale down the level of its aid program to Chile. For the U.S. position is that large-scale external economic assistance to the junta in the immediate future is critical, not only for political reasons but also to create the economic infrastructure for future growth possibilities based on foreign investment. Hence the United States has been critical of the World Bank for "dragging its feet on economic loans" to the military regime in Chile.[85]

The World Bank viewed the military regime in Chile as "preferable, an improvement" over the Allende government and provided the junta with $18.5 million in credits during its first six months in office. However, while the bank's political support of the junta has remained steadfast, it has been critical of some of the specifics of the junta's economic policies.

The World Bank view was that there was more hope of reorganizing the economy on a rational basis under the military government. Inflation, however, continues to be a serious problem. There must be some evidence that they are willing to endure some kind of suffering. Under Allende, the staff of the government increased enormously. Therefore, the government machinery was vastly over-inflated. The military government has made things worse in terms of getting things done because they are more cut off from the bureaucracy than the political parties.

At the beginning the government tried to control everything. If you want to stop inflation, the only way to do it is by running the risk of unemployment. This government has been tough politically, but economically they have been soft. It is true that the people in the slums are suffering, but they are only 10% of the population. All civil servants and people in government jobs have had a good time. This government is unable or unwilling or too stupid to really slow down inflation. So, not really tough enough in the economic sphere. They have been permissive economically.[86]

The World Bank favors the exploitative and dependent capitalist development strategy of the junta, but objects to the way in which the strategy is being implemented.

We did feel that the program they were trying to implement was a consistent one and appeared to contain certain basic decisions that should have led the economy in the right direction. It is the implementation that is the problem. They have failed so far. In macroeconomic terms the policy of austerity has not been implemented.

The Chileans have to implement their announced policies, basically in two respects: they have to get their house in order in financial terms—reduce inflation, balance accounts of most public enterprises and other public sectors—and take decisions as far as investment priorities are concerned. At the moment pretty much the same as under Allende.[87]

The costs of the austerity program being pushed by the World Bank would, needless to say, be borne in large part by the lower classes, the major social base of the Allende government.

The lack of large-scale economic assistance to the military junta from the World Bank in the immediate postcoup period probably stemmed, to some extent, from European objections to the political nature of the new regime. "In the World Bank," observed a State Department economist, "there was very strong opposition to the new government on the part of a number of West European countries." [88] According to a high-ranking CIAP official, "McNamara's position was very much influenced by what the Germans, Swedish, etc., were saying." [89] The West Germans, in particular, expressed considerable dissatisfaction with the repressive aspects of the junta's policies.

> The political appraisal of the political situation by the Germans was very negative in 1974. Agreement between the Chileans and the World Bank was almost ready for approval at the time of the 1973 coup. The decision was suspended and put to the Board of Directors in October 1973. The Germans and some other countries asked for a delay. The same situation happened again in December. There was a suspension of 48 hours. Finally, MacNamara presented it again in February 1974, and it was approved.[90]

The shallow nature of the West German opposition is suggested by the fact that, in spite of a continuation of the policy of repression and terror at home, the military junta was able to successfully conclude bilateral negotiations with West Germany on the rescheduling of Chile's foreign debt in July 1974.

The International Monetary Fund was very supportive of the military junta's economic plight:

> The IMF people who went down to Chile in December 1973 were very sympathetic to the policies of the government and gave full approval to the new economic policies.[91]

The IMF mission's "broad approval" of the junta's economic policies was followed by the approval of a $95 million "standby" credit, a decision which, it was accurately observed, "could open the door for further private financing and also the renegotiation of its sizeable debt." [92] The Economist Intelligence Unit was even more emphatic: "This agreement may be regarded as the key to the whole problem of renegotiating Chile's heavy foreign debt commitments." [93] In March 1974, as we have seen, the debt was renegotiated.

Despite this influx of international capital into Chile since the military coup in September 1973, industrial production has been steadily declining since October "and manufacturers are warning the government that the low purchasing power of consumers may lead to a serious industrial recession." [94] This situation is a pointed indictment, in particular, of the IMF policies regarding the approval of austerity "standby" credits. It is only during the immediate postcoup period that the junta can argue for a favorable industrial performance, but even that is only in comparison with the immediate precoup period characterized by massive economic sabotage. However, although the industrial production index rose from 110.9 in August and 91.7 in September to 138.0 in October, if we compare December 1973 with December 1972 we find that there was a decline in the index from 132.6 to 125.2.[95] Chilean government economists see no signs of a reversal of this present trend.

The Inter-American Committee on the Alliance for Progress (CIAP) issued a detailed analysis of the economic policies of the junta during the last three months of 1973 and was highly critical of the attempt to deal with important fiscal problems.

> Indeed,—according to preliminary estimates—current expenditures for the fourth quarter account for 29.7 percent of the annual total—which is even higher than in the two preceding years. On the other hand, although current income accounts for a percentage higher than that achieved in 1972, it represents only 26.6 percent of the annual total which, as indicated previously, is extremely low. As a result of these factors, the deficit for the fourth quarter accounts for 34.2

percent of the annual total, which would account for 144 percent of the increase in the money supply during that period.[96]

An official of CIAP criticized the IMF's overoptimistic assessment of the Chilean situation:

> Our technical report was much more cautious than the IMF's. Chileans didn't like our position, probably because it didn't represent open support. Our technical position was that they were building a policy and so it was difficult to prove the assumptions, e.g., that entrepreneurs would absorb the cost increase in a very large measure; that people would be satisfied living at very low levels of consumption; assumption that private investment will come; public sector will be able to carry out large investment programs.
> The IMF position openly supported the Chilean program. They were sure, or about sure, that the Chileans would get control of inflation at a low level of 80%. But it is now over 100%. At the same time, we said it would be difficult because we didn't agree with the policies of leaving prices to find their level according to market forces. We were alone at the time and we were criticized by the IMF and the Chilean government.[97]

Similar to the case of Brazil following the 1964 military coup, foreign investors have displayed an initially cautious attitude toward the junta's encouragement to foreign capital to invest in the country. Large-scale foreign investments might be forthcoming once the conditions for capital accumulation and capital export are created. The responsibilities for the infrastructural reorganization of the Chilean economy in order to lay the foundations for dependent capitalist growth have been, and continue to be, undertaken by the U.S. government, the Brazilian government, the international banking community, etc.

In the meantime, the foreign investor community has been pushing the junta for clarification of its policy toward

existing and new foreign investment in Chile. Some private
investors who envisaged an unqualified return to the pre-
Allende status quo have been disappointed. *Business International* commented on the junta's immediate intentions in
November 1973:

> . . . the government does not intend to return completely
> to the pre-Allende status-quo. The military regime feels it
> needs the private sector to help fuel the economy, but it still
> wants to control "strategic industries". . . .[98]

Others have expressed concern over the junta's indecisive
policy regarding the return to private hands of enterprises
nationalized, intervened in, or requisitioned during the
Allende government. To this point, the junta has employed
at least three approaches. On the one hand, companies that
were intervened in or requisitioned have been either handed
back to their original owners, or put up for public sale with
the former owners having the first bid.[99] On the other,
enterprises deemed to have been legally nationalized by the
Allende government (e.g., the U.S.-owned copper companies)
have been kept under state control, subject to compensation
payments to the former owners. The junta has recently
agreed to pay $253 million in compensation to the U.S.
Anaconda Company and $68 million to the U.S. Kennecott
Copper Corporation.[100] However, this concern with the
junta's policy toward existing foreign investment is more
than matched by foreign investor uneasiness over new foreign
investment being subject to Andean Pact restrictions on
profit remittances, the re-export of capital, the nationalization of foreign companies within a certain time period, and
the limits placed on foreign ownership of new enterprises set
up within the Andean area. Although the junta has conven-
iently ignored the Andean Pact controls in the case of a
number of new enterprises, this is viewed by foreign investors
as essentially a short-term solution and no substitute for a

new foreign investment code. A group of foreign businessmen met in Santiago in June 1974, under the auspices of
Business International, to discuss the issue, and "left the
military junta in no doubt at all that the government's
desperate desire for foreign capital will not be satisfied unless
and until it can persuade its partners in the Andean Pact to
modify the paragraphs in the Cartagena Agreement governing foreign investment." [101] Yet, the Brazilian military government has also instituted controls on profit remittances,
etc., but this has taken place in the context of a dynamic
economic growth in which the foreign investor is one of the
major beneficiaries. This suggests that the Chilean junta
cannot count on foreign investment to move the economy; it
must find the means to create a period of growth after which
foreign investors might lose some of their current preoccupa-
tions.

In a word, Chilean development prospects are problematic. To adopt the strategy of the Brazilian generals would
require a permanent repression of the labor force which the
Chilean junta is unlikely to be able to sustain. In comparison
with its Brazilian counterparts, the Chilean working class is
more highly politicized with a long history of political and
economic struggle in support of class demands. Less stringent
policies toward the lower classes and support for the
development of consumer industries for a small Chilean
market would lead to the same mass radical upsurge which
Frei's programs produced between 1964 and 1970, and which
were decisively rejected by the working class. [102] U.S. policy-
makers, however, are adamant on one point:

> I don't think we can afford to have that country revert to
> another Marxist/anti-U.S. regime. We don't have a problem
> with Chile right now. If the regime becomes enfeebled, it will
> become an issue again. Let's say the situation is deteriorating
> and they are not getting themselves functioning in a viable
> economic system. I think that would create circumstances in

which the U.S. government would show less restraint in terms of intervening to support the regime; if the situation became unstable, pragmatic aspects, such that whatever costs involved to U.S. intervening in Latin America, would start to provide strong nonmilitary support.[103]

Economic policies of the imperial centers are largely determined not by abstract criteria of creditworthiness but by the larger politicoeconomic interests embodied in social regimes which buttress capitalist social relations. Our discussion of U.S. policies toward the Frei, Allende, and Pinochet regimes illustrates the interrelation between the needs of U.S. capitalism and public policy; the bonds between U.S. policy and Chilean propertied groups; the primacy of defending both U.S. and Chilean propertied interests over and against any commitment to parliamentary institutions. The long-term consequences of these international structural bonds and policy commitments suggest that any effort to isolate the purely national (Chilean) or international (U.S.) factors affecting the future development of Chile is a fruitless undertaking. The long-term trend, as indicated by the massive infusion of external financial capital, is for the immersion of Chile into a web of economic relations that will in effect shape the contours and thrust of its politico-economic project. Whatever national identity the Chilean ruling class possessed, and whatever its role in mediating external influence in the past, present developments suggest that image is no longer adequate. The "new Chile" which is emerging from the wreckage of the September 1973 coup increasingly resembles the traditional dependent Latin American country.

7
Conclusion

The U.S. government policy of prolonged confrontation with the Allende government in order to undermine its capacity to govern, and effect its demise, originated from within the offices of Henry Kissinger and the National Security Council. The NSC located the Allende electoral victory in terms of its future negative impact on U.S. political and economic goals in Latin America, and then proceeded to decentralize the implementation of the overall strategy among the appropriate government agencies. At the critical conjuncture, however, it returned to center stage to give its final approval. The military coup followed.

The Chilean coup eliminated the core threat to continued U.S. hegemony in Latin America. The restoration of a client regime in Chile had immediate short-term consequences. In October, Secretary of State Kissinger called for a "new dialogue" between the United States and Latin America to re-examine the nature of the relationship. U.S. officials stated that "this was [Kissinger's] first policy statement on Latin America and was meant to signal the start of a major effort by the Administration to work out a fresh approach to the problems in the hemisphere. . . ."[1] The creation of a U.S.-Brazilian "co-prosperity" policy in Latin America is likely. Chile is merely one of the pieces within this larger picture.

As the policies of Chile's military rulers unfold, differences have already appeared among the anti-Allende forces in the United States as well as in Chile. The differences are not insignificant insofar as they reflect not only changes in personnel (civilian vs. military), but different positions regarding forms of political rule, the role of the military, and socioeconomic policy. What appeared as a united effort between political parties and military officers to prevent the "communization of Chile" is no longer visible. The stronger party to the coup, the military, has discarded its political associates, the Frei-led Christian Democrats (PDC), and feels free to impose its own policies through direct representation in the government.[2] In this the military has the support of the smaller upper-class-based National Party and the terrorist ultraright Fatherland and Liberty group (together representing about 20 percent of the electorate).

Through terror, the military was hoping to erase social pressure from the Left; by political exclusion and cooptation, to definitively divide the Christian Democrats; by offering important posts and rewards to the National Party and businessmen, to consolidate an administrative apparatus capable of imposing "discipline" on labor (with the aid of terror), and securing the cooperation of business; and with an open-door policy to foreign investment, to stimulate foreign loans, credits, and investment to stimulate economic recovery. The "Brazilian Model" is being projected in Chile over the corpses of 20,000 workers: salaries and wages are being effectively lowered, prices increased, currency devalued, enterprises returned to private owners, and the conditions created for externally induced expansion at the cost of the poor. In the near future, the middle class, business groups, and industrialists will suffer the invasion of large-scale foreign capital which, in the name of efficiency, will eliminate many of those who supported the coup. Large sectors of the petite bourgeoisie who were in the streets calling for the coup will not be its beneficiaries. As in Brazil, the generals and their economic advisors are looking toward the multinational corporation and the international banks to reorganize the economy: they, too, have no confidence in the "entrepreneurial" capacity of the national bourgeoisie, in much the same way they do not trust their bourgeois "democrats" organized in the PDC to restore and maintain capitalist law and order. If a permanent military-corporate structure is the political instrument of the leaders of the coup, large-scale foreign enterprises are their answer to the economic problems facing the country.

The U.S. government long ago gave up the idea that a parliamentary facade is a necessary accompaniment of capitalist development in Latin America. The incapacity of parliamentary regimes to offer guarantees against radicalism and nationalism and their inability to create favorable conditions for foreign investment have for some time provoked U.S. policy-makers and economic influentials into rethinking the "best" political formula to serve their interests in Latin America. Brazil provided the test case: while Frei was incapable of preventing a Marxist from winning the presidential elections in Chile, the military dictators in Brazil were attracting loans and investments from all the centers of world capitalism. While U.S. Ambassador Korry was complaining that he had to tell Frei how to put his pants on (figuratively speaking, we assume), the Brazilian military government had practically eliminated all guerrillas, trade unions, strikes, and wage demands, thus creating an industrialists' paradise. Whatever promises Frei might have had from Washington before the coup, he had clearly revealed himself as someone the United States could not trust to take over after Allende, despite his espousal of the coup and its terror tactics. After all, it was the military that was willing to bloody its hands, and therefore it was the military which would be willing to take the appropriate measures after the coup to prevent a resurgence of leftism. With the breakdown of the constituted order, and the emergence of a leftist under-ground, U.S. policy-makers did not believe that Frei would be able to handle the new situation and provide the kind of security to foreign capital that the military could offer, despite the massive and bloody purge. Only a few dissident and peripheral voices of the liberal establishment (*New York Times*, Ford Foundation, *Washington Post*, etc.) felt that the military purge created a secure basis for a return to parliamentary order and the restoration of Eduardo Frei. The mainstream of U.S. officialdom, the bankers, the international financial agencies, the State Department, the National Security Council, and the multinational corpora-tions have already begun to back the military, its policies, and its leadership. At best they viewed Frei as a useful but temporary ally on the road to power, suspect for his earlier failure to disregard the democratic verdict of the Chilean people. Now, in the new situation, they are unlikely to offer him more than an honorific secondary post or quiet retire-ment. The military is not a caretaker government but a permanent political force,[3] the dominant political force in a Chile backed by U.S. economic resources and adapting the Brazilian development strategy to Chilean conditions.

One of the crucial long-term problems facing U.S. policy-makers at the highest level (what can be more accurately described as the historical problems facing the world capital-ist system), is the creation of the conditions for economic expansion through private accumulation in dependent capi-talist societies. The political formulas or frameworks which are best suited for the capitalist problematic vary with time and place, but each political experience is compared and evaluated in terms of its efficiency in achieving its historic goal. In operational terms the problems of economic expansion and accumulation are essentially political in a double sense: at the level of the state there must exist a dominant political elite willing to subordinate the machinery of government to controlling the working and peasant classes (minimizing their political effectiveness, therefore lowering their "social costs," i.e., salaries, wages, etc.), and a political orientation which deliberately opens the country to the free flow of capital, especially foreign capital. The existence of the quasi-totalitarian state is especially necessary in those countries which have experienced a high degree of social mobilization: for there is an inverse relationship between externally induced growth and social mobilization: the greater the degree of the latter the less likely the former will occur.

Externally induced expansion and accumulation (which appears to be the only source for whatever large-scale industrialization has taken place within underdeveloped capitalist countries) is dependent upon an authoritarian political framework which can reinforce the requisite social conditions. These social requisites for private accumulation and expansion in dependent capitalist societies include a demobilized working class, nonexistent or weak economic nationalist political forces, the elimination or curtailment of wage demands and massive and extensive social welfare programs, and controlled or managed trade unions (Falangist-type syndicates). The administrative structure best suited to preserve or enhance those conditions is likely to recruit its top personnel from the propertied groups and technocrats which serve them. The interpenetration of civilian and military bureaucracy is likely especially at the highest and middle levels, thus strengthening the power and capacity of the administration to impose its policies on those who benefit least from them. These social requisites and administrative structures are linked through the socioeconomic policies of the military-political elite: a deliberate policy of wage and salary reductions of workers is promoted to reconcentrate income in the hands of the foreign and domestic propertied classes. Sharp increases in prices and profits are allowed far in excess of the increases in wages; wage workers in fact suffer a relative and absolute decline in real living standards.

The whole process in Chile began with the disaggregation of the state—the creation of a client group among the military. Since seizing power it sought to recast the whole state organization into an administrative instrument for realizing the social and political conditions for externally induced expansion. The process of reintegrating Chile within the financial and economic networks of imperialism has proceeded at a fairly rapid rate only because the internal political controls and repression have re-established confidence among the international bankers (though corporate investors appear still to have reservations, especially those investors who would generate new capital). The political problems that U.S. policy-makers faced under Allende (of taking political measures to ensure that Chile was reintegrated back into the capitalist world) have been at least temporarily successfully resolved. What remains very doubtful is the medium- and long-term durability of a regime whose private sector has in the past shown little inclination to accumulate and invest capital for long-term expansion. And Chile, unlike Brazil, has neither the large internal market nor the passive work force that makes the latter so attractive to the multinationals. In any case, Chile may have had its bourgeois counterrevolution too late: if one has Brazil from which to expand throughout the region and beyond, what function can Chile play within the larger imperial design? While Chile may wish to copy "the Brazilian model," there does not appear to be, from the multinational perspective, any need to duplicate functions. What appears more likely is that Chile will be relegated to the role of raw material and mineral exporter within the larger imperial division of labor.[4] The military's job will be to keep Chile producing within this global pattern.

Appendix

The following tables illustrate the close relationship between United States (and "international") foreign aid and the nature of the social regime to which it is directed. The periods of expansiveness coincide with regimes whose policies coincide with the needs of U.S. capitalism; the periods of restrictive financial assistance coincide with populist-nationalist or democratic socialist governments. These conclusions, drawn from comparisons between Brazil and Chile during the Allende period, are substantiated by comparisons within countries during different time periods: the Goulart period/ post-1964; the Allende period/Frei period. U.S. aid to elected nationalist and democratic socialist governments in Brazil and Chile is further diminished if we take into account *who the recipients of that aid were within the country*. Prior to the military dictatorship of 1964 in Brazil the federal structure of government provided a great deal of autonomy to the state governments: a substantial amount if not the bulk of U.S. financial resources were funneled into states controlled by right-wing pro-coup governors like Carlos Lacerda. In Chile the pluralistic structure during the Allende period allowed the United States to channel funds into the Catholic university and the military, both institutions dominated by the anti-Allende forces. While it is obvious that

U.S. aid policy is directed to bolster and promote pro-U.S. military dictatorships as opposed to democratic governments, what is less obvious, but equally important, is that the aid which is selectively directed toward the democratic governments is utilized to undermine the executive authority and create political alliances with opposition social and political forces.

Table A–1
Brazil:
Foreign Aid from Selected U.S. Government Agencies
and International Organizations ($M)
in the Goulart Period

	1962	1963	1962–1963 Total
U.S. AID	85.1	86.5	171.6
U.S. Food for Peace (PL 480)	72.5	47.9	120.4
U.S. Military Assistance	49.6	17.5	67.1
U.S. Export-Import Bank	9.3	—	9.3
IBRD (World Bank)	—	—	—
IDB (Inter-American Development Bank)	25.6	18.6	44.2

Source: U.S. Agency for International Development, *U.S. Overseas Loans and Grants and Assistance from International Organizations,* July 1, 1945–June 30, 1973. Statistics and Reports Division, Office of Financial Management, AID, May 1974, pp. 40, 182; U.S. Agency for International Development, *U.S. Overseas Loans and Grants and Assistance from International Organizations,* July 1, 1945–June 30, 1971, in *NACLA's Latin America and Empire Report* ("Brazil: Development for Whom?"), April 1973, p. 16; U.S., Congress, House, Committee on Foreign Affairs, *Development Assistance to Latin America,* April 14, 1971, Committee Print (Washington, U.S. Government Printing Office, 1971), p. 8.

Table A–2
Brazil:
Credits and Loans from U.S. Government
Agencies and International Institutions in 1964 ($M)*

	Precoup Jan. 1–March 31	Postcoup April 1–Dec. 31
From U.S. government agencies	18.7	407.8
From international institutions	—	82.3

* Fiscal year 1964 Military Sales from U.S. Government = $23.4 million.
Source: U.S. Department of the Treasury, *Foreign Credits*, by the United States Government, as of December 31, 1969 (Washington: U.S. Government Printing Office, 1970), pp. 98–100.

Table A–3
Brazil:
Foreign Aid from Selected U.S. Government Agencies
and International Organizations ($M)
in the Military Government Period

	1965	1966	1967	1968	1969	1970	1971	1972	1973	Total 1965–1973
U.S. AID	234.9	243.7	214.9	193.8	12.4	88.0	79.4	12.1	40.6	1,119.8
U.S. Food for Peace (PL 480)	24.6	79.1	21.6	82.9	10.2	62.4	35.1	5.7	9.6	331.2
U.S. Military Assistance	11.2	30.6	32.6	36.1	0.8	0.8	12.1	20.8	17.7	162.7
U.S. Export-Import Bank	6.0	16.9	30.0	50.8	27.9	63.2	75.0	299.8	142.3	711.9
IBRD	79.5	49.0	100.6	61.9	74.9	205.0	160.4	437.0	133.7	1,302.2
IDB	80.4	87.2	125.7	76.6	99.8	160.6	119.9	210.1	180.2	1,140.5

Source: See Table A–1.

Table A-4
Chile:
Foreign Aid from Selected U.S. Government Agencies
and International Organizations ($M)
in the Frei Period

	1964	1965	1966	1967	1968	1969	1970	Total 1964–1970
U.S. AID	78.5	99.0	93.2	15.5	57.9	35.4	18.0	397.5
U.S. Food for Peace (PL 480)	26.9	14.2	14.4	7.9	23.0	15.0	7.2	108.6
U.S. Military Assistance	9.8	8.0	10.2	4.2	7.8	11.7	0.8	52.5
U.S. Export-Import Bank	15.3	8.2	0.1	212.3	13.4	28.7	—	278.0
IBRD	22.6	4.4	2.7	60.0	—	11.6	19.3	120.6
IDB	16.6	4.9	62.2	31.0	16.5	31.9	45.6	208.7

Source: U.S. Agency for International Development, *U.S. Overseas Loans and Grants and Assistance from International Organizations,* July 1, 1945–June 30, 1973. Statistics and Reports Division, Office of Financial Management, AID, May 1974, pp. 41, 183; U.S. Agency for International Development, *U.S. Overseas Loans and Grants and Assistance from International Organizations,* July 1, 1945–June 30, 1970, in NACLA, *New Chile,* 1972, pp. 48–49; U.S. AID and Predecessor Agencies, *The Economic Assistance Programs,* April 3, 1948–June 30, 1968. Statistics and Reports Division, Office of Program and Policy Coordination, AID, March 28, 1969, p. 29.

Table A–5
Chile:
Foreign Aid from Selected U.S. Government Agencies
and International Organizations ($M)
in the Allende Period

	1971	1972	1973	Total 1971–1973
U.S. AID	1.5	1.0	0.8	3.3
U.S. Food for Peace (PL 480)	6.3	5.9	2.5	14.7
U.S. Military Assistance	5.7	12.3	15.0	33.0
U.S. Export-Import Bank	—	1.6	3.1	4.7
IBRD	—	—	—	—
IDB	12.0	2.1	5.2	17.3

Source: See Table A–4.

Table A–6
Chile:
Foreign Aid from U.S. Government Agencies and
International Organizations ($M)
for the Military Government
September 1973+

See Table 3.

Notes

Preface

1. A statement made at a meeting of the Committee of 40 in June 1970, two months before the Chilean presidential elections. Quoted in Seymour M. Hersh, "Censored Matter in Book About C.I.A. Said to Have Related Chile Activities," *New York Times*, September 11, 1974, p. 14.
2. Richard Nixon, *U.S. Foreign Policy for the 1970s*, A Report to the Congress, February 25, 1971 (Washington: U.S. Government Printing Office, 1971), pp. 53–54.
3. U.S., Congress, Senate, Committee on Foreign Relations, Subcommittee on Multinational Corporations, *Multinational Corporations and United States Foreign Policy, Part 1*, 93rd Cong., March 20, 21, 22, 27, 28, 29, and April 4, 1973 (Washington: U.S. Government Printing Office, 1973), p. 281.
4. Ibid., p. 402.
5. Quoted in Lawrence Stern, "Perjury Inquiry Urged on Chile Data," *Washington Post*, September 17, 1974, p. A7. This statement was made by Kissinger during his confirmation hearings to be Secretary of State in September 1973, but was deleted from the published hearings.
6. U.S., Congress, Senate, Committee on Foreign Relations, *Nomination of Henry A. Kissinger, Part 2* (Executive Hear-

ings), September 17, 1973 (Washington: U.S. Government Printing Office, 1973), p. 303.

7. *Department of State Bulletin*, October 8, 1973, p. 465.

8. U.S., Congress, House, Committee on Foreign Affairs, Subcommittee on Inter-American Affairs and on International Organizations and Movements, *Human Rights in Chile*, 93rd Cong., 2nd Sess., December 7, 1973, May 7, 23, June 11, 12, and 18, 1974 (Washington: U.S. Government Printing Office, 1974) pp. 123, 136.

9. Statement made during hearings before the House Foreign Affairs Committee, June 5, 1974.

10. "Transcript of President's News Conference on Foreign and Domestic Matters," *New York Times*, September 17, 1974, p. 22.

11. Quoted in Seymour M. Hersh, "C.I.A. Chief Tells House of $8 Million Campaign Against Allende in '70–73," *New York Times*, September 8, 1974, p. 26.

12. Letter from Senator J. W. Fulbright to Congressman Michael J. Harrington, July 26, 1974.

13. See "Transcript of President's News Conference on Foreign and Domestic Matters," p. 22; Bernard Gwertzman, "Kissinger Tells of Hope to Widen Ties with Soviet," *New York Times*, September 20, 1974, pp. 1, 18. The Ford/Kissinger concern with preserving the opposition media from imminent destruction had no foundation in fact. The Allende government, throughout its tenure in office, "neither owned nor censored the media, and its political opposition had a decisive advantage in terms of magazines, radio, television, and movies." See Patricia Fagen, "The Media in Allende's Chile," *Journal of Communication*, Winter 1974, pp. 59–70. *El Mercurio*, the principal opposition newspaper in Chile, was closed down only once during the Allende period (for less than a week) after it had published an editorial advocating insurrection against the government. See Tad Szulc, "Where President Ford Is Wrong," *New Republic*, September 28, 1974, p. 14.

14. Quoted in Seymour M. Hersh, "Kissinger Called Chile Strategist," *New York Times*, September 15, 1974, pp. 1, 19.

15. Quoted in ibid.

16. Quoted in "Doubt on U.S. Role in Chile Recalled," *New York Times*, October 17, 1974, p. 9.

17. Quoted in Seymour M. Hersh, "Washington Said to Have Authorized a 'Get-Rougher' Policy in Chile in '71," *New York Times*, September 24, 1974, p. 2.

18. See Seymour M. Hersh, "C.I.A. Is Linked to Strike in Chile that Beset Allende," *New York Times*, September 20, 1974, pp. 1, 10.

19. Quoted in Seymour M. Hersh, "Kissinger Said to Rebuke U.S. Ambassador to Chile," *New York Times*, September 27, 1974, p.18.

Introduction

1. John H. Crimmins, Acting Assistant Secretary of State for Inter-American Affairs, before a House Foreign Affairs Subcommittee. See U.S., Congress, House, Committee on Foreign Affairs, Subcommittee on Inter-American Affairs, *United States-Chilean Relations*, 93rd Cong., 1st sess., March 6, 1973 (Washington: U.S. Government Printing Office, 1973), p. 15.

2. Jack Kubisch, Assistant Secretary of State for Inter-American Affairs, before the House Foreign Affairs Committee, September 20, 1973. See *Department of State Bulletin*, October 8, 1973, pp. 465–466.

3. Henry Kissinger, Secretary of State-designate, before the Senate Committee on Foreign Relations. See U.S., Congress, Senate, Committee on Foreign Relations, *Nomination of Henry A. Kissinger, Part 2*, p. 304.

4. Paul E. Sigmund, "The 'Invisible Blockade' and the Overthrow of Allende," *Foreign Affairs*, January 1974, pp. 337–339.

5. Henry Landsberger, "Answers to Some Questions About the Military Coup in Chile" (unpublished paper; University of North Carolina at Chapel Hill, September 30, 1973), pp. 16, 22, 23, Appendix 3.

6. Interview No. 3–4, U.S. Department of the Treasury, Washington, D.C., June 10, 1974.

7. Paul N. Rosenstein-Rodan, "Allende's Big Failing: Incompetence," *New York Times*, June 16, 1974, p. E12.

Rosenstein-Rodan, a former advisor to the Frei government, presents a totally *incompetent* account of the Allende period, which overlooks almost all of its most essential aspects. During the Allende period, incompetence was never an issue, given the large number of qualified individuals who were attracted to, and joined, the administration. What were critical issues, and what Rosenstein-Rodan does not discuss, are foreign economic pressures; CIA covert activities in Chile; internal sabotage by opposition groups; the impact of the decline in international copper prices; the role of the opposition-dominated congress in blocking attempts at responsible fiscal financing by the Allende government, etc. Instead, we are subjected to simplistic distortions such as the following:

> The collapse [of the Allende government] came with the truckers' strike. Those drivers employed by large firms had benefited from Mr. Allende's initial reforms, but many of the truckers were small, self-employed entrepreneurs. The strike began as a normal collective bargaining dispute, but rapidly acquired a political tone. The lower middle class was entering into a revolutionary euphoria of its own. The truckers wanted guarantees that the expropriations would not be applied to them. Eventually, their goal became President Allende's resignation.

More objective observers have been able to separate fact from fiction in discussing the Chilean experience with democratic socialism.

8. "Expropriation itself is an issue," observed a National Security Council official, "in that it bothers people domestically for ideological reasons." Interview No. 2–18, National Security Council, Washington, D.C., August 14, 1973.

9. Figures taken from a study prepared by CORFO (the Chilean Development Corporation) in August 1972, as cited in Kyle Steenland, "Two Years of Popular Unity in Chile: A Balance Sheet," *New Left Review*, March–April 1973, p. 14.

10. James Petras and Robert LaPorte, Jr., "U.S. Response to Economic Nationalism in Chile," in James Petras, ed., *Latin*

America: From Dependence to Revolution (New York: John Wiley and Sons, 1973), pp. 219–222.

11. James D. Cockcroft, Henry Frundt, and Dale L. Johnson, "The Multi-nationals," in Dale L. Johnson, ed., *The Chilean Road to Socialism* (New York: Doubleday Anchor, 1973), p. 13.

12. "Chile: Facing the Blockade," *NACLA's Latin America and Empire Report*, January 1973, pp. 20–21, 26–27; *Chile Hoy*, August 11–17, 1972, p. 16.

13. Economist Intelligence Unit, *Quarterly Economic Review of Chile*, no. 2, May 1973, p. 10.

1. The U.S. Role in Chile, 1964–1970

1. Federico G. Gil, *The Political System of Chile* (Boston: Houghton Mifflin Co., 1966), pp. 242–243.

2. Laurence Stern, "U.S. Helped Beat Allende in 1964," *Washington Post*, April 6, 1973, pp. A1, A12.

3. Quoted in ibid.

4. Laurence Stern, "Ex-Spy to Give Detailed Account of Covert CIA Operations," *Washington Post*, July 11, 1974, p. A3.

5. Quoted in ibid. According to an ITT memorandum, "The U.S. government sponsored and paid for special political polls, analyzed Frei's campaign, gave him extraordinary consolation and comfort, all under the friendly aegis of then U.S. Ambassador Ralph Dungan." See U.S., Congress, Senate, Committee on Foreign Relations, Subcommittee on Multi-national Corporations, *Multinational Corporations and United States Foreign Policy, Part 2*, 93rd Cong., March 20, 21, 22, 27, 28, 29, and April 4, 1973 (Washington: U.S. Government Printing Office, 1973), p. 704.

6. Quoted in David J. Morris, *We Must Make Haste Slowly: The Process of Revolution in Chile* (New York: Vintage Books, 1973), p. 56.

7. See Miles D. Wolpin, *Cuban Foreign Policy and Chilean Politics* (Lexington, Mass.: D. C. Heath and Co., 1972), p. 92.

8. U.S., Congress, House, Committee on Banking and Currency, *Latin American Economic Study*, 91st Cong., 1st sess., Octo-

ber 1969 (Washington: U.S. Government Printing Office, 1969), p. 19; U.S., Congress, Senate, Committee on Foreign Relations, Subcommittee on Multinational Corporations, *Multinational Corporations and United States Foreign Policy, Part 1*, p. 113.

9. U.S., Congress, Senate, Committee on Government Operations, Subcommittee on Foreign Aid Expenditures, *United States Foreign Aid in Action: A Case Study*, 89th Cong., 2nd sess. (Washington: U.S. Government Printing Office, 1966), pp. 50–51.

10. U.S., Congress, House, Committee on Foreign Affairs, *Development Assistant to Latin America 1961–1970*, April 14, 1971, Committee Print (Washington: U.S. Government Printing Office, 1971), pp. 9–10 (Tables 9 and 10).

11. U.S., Congress, Senate, *United States Foreign Aid in Action: A Case Study*, p. 103.

12. Ibid., p. 106. In a post-election audit, AID also found that between $60,000 and $70,000 worth of U.S. food supplies donated to CARITAS (the major social welfare agency of the Catholic Church in Chile) had been "diverted to Christian Democratic campaigners during the campaign." See Wolpin, p. 345.

13. Harvey S. Perloff, *Alliance for Progress* (Baltimore, Maryland: Johns Hopkins Press, 1969), p. 230 (Table A–3).

14. Quoted in Laurence Stern, "U.S. Helped Beat Allende in 1964," pp. A1, A12. Also see Jerome Levinson and Juan de Onis, *The Alliance That Lost Its Way* (Chicago: Quadrangle Books, 1972), p. 91.

15. Joan M. Nelson, *Aid, Influence, and Foreign Policy* (New York: Macmillan Co., 1968), p. 99.

16. U.S., Congress, House, Committee on Foreign Affairs, *The Overseas Private Investment Corporation*, 93rd Cong., 1st sess., Committee Print, September 4, 1973 (Washington: U.S. Government Printing Office, 1973), p. 95.

17. Quoted in ibid.

18. "Excerpts from AID's Presentation of the Case for Increased Aid to Chile in the Months Preceding Allende's Election," *Inter-American Economic Affairs*, Winter 1970, p. 91. AID

requested a $9.3 million increase in aid over the 1970 authorization.

19. Ibid., p. 91.

Chile: Annual Growth Rates of GDP, 1961–1969 (%)

1961	1962	1963	1964	1965	1966	1967	1968	1969
6.2	5.0	4.7	4.2	5.0	7.0	2.3	2.9	3.3

See Organization of American States, Inter-American Economic and Social Council, Inter-American Committee on the Alliance for Progress, *Domestic Efforts and Needs for External Financing for the Development of Chile*, CIAP [Inter-American Committee on the Alliance for Progress] Subcommittee on Chile, April 24–28, 1972 (Washington, D.C., OEA/Ser. H/XIV, CIAP/t41, April 21, 1972), p. 102.

20. See Agency for International Development, *U.S. Overseas Loans and Grants and Assistance from International Organizations*, July 1, 1945–June 30, 1972 (Washington: Office of Financial Management, Statistics and Reports Division, AID, May 1973), pp. 42, 181.

21. Economist Intelligence Unit, *Quarterly Economic Review of Chile*, Annual Supplement, 1973, p. 15.

2. U.S. Policy and the Election of Allende, September–November 1970

1. U.S., Congress, Senate, Committee on Foreign Relations, Subcommittee on Multinational Corporations, *The International Telephone and Telegraph Company and Chile, 1970–71*, Committee Print, June 21, 1973, 93rd Cong. (Washington: U.S. Government Printing Office, 1973), p. 3.

2. U.S., Congress, Senate, *Multinational Corporations and United States Foreign Policy, Part 1*, p. 290.

3. Ibid., pp. 291–292. A high-level Treasury Department official described the 1970 election as "a presumably democratic type of election," Interview No. 2–19, U.S. Department of the Treasury, Washington, D.C., August 13, 1973.

4. U.S., Congress, Senate, *Multinational Corporations and United States Foreign Policy, Part 2*, pp. 542–543. Also see,

Tad Szulc, "Briefing on Chile Disturbs Chile," *New York Times*, September 23, 1970, p. 13. Kissinger was also quoted as saying: "I don't see why we need to stand by and watch a country go communist due to the irresponsibility of its own people," in Seymour M. Hersh, "Censored Matter in Book About CIA. Said to Have Related Chile Activities," *New York Times*, September 11, 1974, p. 14.

5. U.S., Congress, Senate, *The International Telephone and Telegraph Company and Chile*, 1970–71, p. 9.
6. "Business in Chile Braces for Storm After Election Victory by Marxist Allende," *Business Latin America*, September 10, 1970, p. 290.
7. U.S., Congress, Senate, *Multinational Corporations and United States Foreign Policy*, Part 2, pp. 801–803.
8. Ibid., pp. 599–600. Similar information was also conveyed to Charles Meyer, Assistant Secretary of State for Inter-American Affairs. According to McCone, the original directive from ITT chairman Harold S. Geneen was quite specific:

> What he told me at that time was that he was prepared to put as much as a million dollars in support of any plan that was adopted by the government for the purpose of bringing about a coalition of the opposition to Allende so that when confirmation was up, which was some months later, this coalition would be united and deprive Allende of his position. (Ibid., *Part I*, p. 102)

ITT memorandums were highly critical of the refusal of other U.S. corporations with economic interests in Chile to support ITT's policy.

> Repeated calls to firms such as GM, Ford, and banks in California and New York have drawn no offers of help. All have some sort of excuse. (Ibid., *Part 2*, p. 643)

> Practically no progress has been made in trying to get American business to cooperate in some way so as to bring on economic chaos. (Ibid., p. 644)

This division, however, was essentially short-term and a question of tactics rather than policy. A number of U.S. corporations were prepared to withhold action until after the results of compensation negotiations with the Allende government for any expropriated properties.

9. Ibid., pp. 608–609.
10. Ibid., *Part 1*, pp. 250–251.
11. Ibid., *Part 2*, p. 622.
12. Ibid., p. 644.
13. Ibid., p. 659. Ex-General Viaux was convicted of conspiring in the assassination of the constitutionalist commander in chief of the Chilean armed forces, General Rene Schneider, in October 1970.
14. Ibid., pp. 665–666.
15. Ibid., pp. 720–721.
16. U.S. policy-makers distinguished between the more "neanderthal" aspects of ITT's strategy (e.g., "public threats"), and those aspects, such as economic coercion, which were more in line with the new low profile policy. Interview No. 2–16, National Security Council, Washington, D.C. August 9, 1973.

3. The National Security Council and the Initial U.S. Response to Allende

1. Richard Nixon, *United States Foreign Policy in the 1970s*, A Report to the Congress, February 18, 1970 (Washington, D.C.: U.S. Government Printing Office, 1970), p. 19.
2. Robert Semple, Jr., "Nixon to Revive Council's Power," *New York Times*, January 1, 1969, pp. 1–10.
3. Quoted in ibid.
4. Peter Grose, "Kissinger Gains a Key Authority in Foreign Policy," *New York Times*, February 5, 1969, pp. 1, 8.
5. John P. Leacacos, "Kissinger's Apparat," *Foreign Policy*, Winter 1971–72, p. 7.
6. Quoted in William Beecher, "New Panel to Coordinate Defense Outlay and Policy," *New York Times*, November 29, 1969, p. 16.

7. Leacacos, pp. 7–8. The Committee of Forty authorized a CIA fund of $400,000 at its June 1970 meeting to discuss the Chilean situation, to be used to support anti-Allende media operations. However, Colby refused to divulge the extent to which CIA operations in Chile were authorized by the Committee of Forty.

> We have had . . . various relationships over the years in Chile with various groups. In some cases this was approved by the National Security Council and it has meant some assistance to them. (Quoted in Tad Szulc, "The View from Langley," *Washington Post*, October 21, 1973, p. C5)

8. Ibid. Also see comments of U. Alexis Johnson, Under-Secretary of State for Political Affairs, on the operation of the National Security Council, in U.S., Congress, House, Committee on Foreign Affairs, Subcommittee on National Security Council and Scientific Developments, *National Security Policy and the Changing World Power Alignments*, 92nd Cong., 2nd sess., May 24, 31, June 7, 14, 21, 28, and August 8, 1972 (Washington: U.S. Government Printing Office, 1972), p. 375.

9. "Nixon Reorganizes Intelligence Work," *New York Times*, November 6, 1971, p. 14; Benjamin Welles, "Helms Told to Cut Global Expenses," *New York Times*, November 7, 1971, p. 5.

10. Interview No. 2–16.

11. Popular Unity program, as printed in North American Congress on Latin America, *New Chile*, 1972, p. 130.

12. Senator Edward M. Kennedy, *Address to the Chicago Council on Foreign Relations*, October 12, 1971 (Washington, D.C.: Office of Senator Edward M. Kennedy), pp. 2–3.

13. Richard Nixon, *U.S. Foreign Policy for the 1970s*, A Report to the Congress, February 25, 1971 (Washington, D.C.: U.S. Government Printing Office, 1971), pp. 53–54. Allende, in reply, noted that "the interests of the United States and the interests of Latin America fundamentally have nothing in common." Nonetheless, he emphasized that Chile "wants to maintain cordial and cooperative relations with all nations in

the world and most particularly with the United States. . . ."
See Salvador Allende, *Chile's Road to Socialism* (Baltimore:
Penguin Books, 1973), pp. 105, 106.

14. Jacob K. Javits, "OPIC, New Hope for U.S. Participation in
the Second Development Decade," *Address to the International Management Division of the American Management
Association*, New York, February 1, 1971 (Washington, D.C.:
Office of Senator Jacob K. Javits), pp. 3–4.

15. Interview No. 2–16.

16. Quoted from a memorandum prepared by Ronald R. Raddatz
of the Bank of America, which summarized the initial meeting
of the Ad Hoc Committee in January 1971. Representatives of
the Bank of America, Anaconda, Kennecott, W. R. Grace Co.,
Pfizer Chemical, and Ralston Purina attended the meeting.
See U.S., Congress, Senate, *Multinational Corporations and
United States Foreign Policy, Part 1*, p. 44.

17. U.S., Congress, Senate, *Multinational Corporations and
United States Foreign Policy, Part 2*, pp. 1009–1010, and *Part
1*, p. 44.

18. Ibid.

19. Ibid., pp. 46–47. By mid-January 1971, ITT officials had visited,
or made appointments with, U.S. government officials in the
Departments of State, Treasury, and Commerce, the National
Security Council, and the Office of Emergency Preparedness,
as well as with congressional personnel. See ibid., *Part 2*,
p. 1052.

20. "An Economic Team from Chile Puts Its Case in Washington
for Continued Investment by Foreigners," *New York Times*,
February 25, 1971, p. 11.

21. Juan de Onis, "U.S. Cancellation of Visit by Enterprise Stirs
Chile," *New York Times*, March 7, 1971, p. 3. According to a
subsequent report, President Nixon overruled the Pentagon
and some senior State Department officials in canceling the
visit. See Benjamin Welles, "4 U.S. Officers to go to Chilean
Fete," *New York Times*, March 18, 1971, p. 3. Throughout this
early period, Allende's response to U.S. policy was moderate
and restrained. He continued to reiterate Chile's desire to

maintain friendly relations with the United States, and stressed that Chile would "never provide a military base that might be used against the United States. . . ." Quoted in *Facts on File*, April 1–7, 1971, p. 257.

4. U.S. Policy Toward Chile in the Context of the Brazilian and Peruvian Models

1. Interview No. 3–3, Council on International Economic Policy, Washington, D.C., June 7, 1974.
2. Inter-American Development Bank, *Social Progress Trust Fund*, Fourth Annual Report 1964 (Washington: February 26, 1965), p. 177.
3. Octavio Ianni, *Crisis in Brazil* (New York: Columbia University Press, 1971), p. 118. On Goulart's lack of a radical alternative, also see Andre Gunder Frank, "The Goulart Ouster: Brazil in Perspective," *The Nation*, April 27, 1964, p. 409.
4. Ianni, p. 129.
5. Stern, "Ex-Spy to Give Detailed Account of Covert CIA Operations," p. A3.
6. Peter D. Bell, "Brazilian-American Relations," in Riordan Roett, ed., *Brazil in the Sixties* (Nashville: Vanderbilt University Press, 1972), p. 95.
7. U.S. Agency for International Development, *U.S. Overseas Loans and Grants and Assistance from International Organizations*, July 1, 1945-June 30, 1973. (Washington: AID, Office of Financial Management, Statistics and Reports Division, May 1974), p. 182.
8. Testimony of William A. Ellis, Director of USAID in Brazil, May 5, 1971. U.S., Congress, Senate, Committee on Foreign Relations, Subcommittee on Western Hemisphere Affairs, *United States Policies and Programs in Brazil*, 92nd Cong., 1st sess., May 4, 5, and 11, 1971 (Washington: U.S. Government Printing Office, 1971), p. 250.
9. Quoted in Carlos F. Diaz-Alejandro, "Some Aspects of the Brazilian Experience with Foreign Aid," in Jagdish N.

Bhagwati et. al., eds., *Trade, Balance of Payments and Growth* (New York: American Elsevier Publishing Co., 1971), p. 452.

10. U.S. General Accounting Office, *Review of Administration of United States Assistance for Capital Development Projects in Brazil*, Report to the Congress by the Comptroller General of the United States, Washington, D.C., B-133283, May 16, 1968, pp. 2, 5.

11. Ibid., p. 70.

12. Ibid., p. 59.

13. Ibid., p. 70.

14. Thomas E. Skidmore, *Politics in Brazil 1930–1964* (London: Oxford University Press, 1967), p. 271.

15. Ibid., pp. 270–271.

16. See Tad Szulc, "U.S. May Abandon Efforts to Deter Latin Dictators," *New York Times*, March 19, 1964, pp. 1, 2.

17. See Ronald Radosh, *American Labor and United States Foreign Policy* (New York: Random House, 1969), especially pp. 393–405.

18. Ibid., p. 425.

19. Quoted in Robert H. Dockery, "Labor Policies and Programs," in U.S., Congress, Senate, Committee on Foreign Relations, Subcommittee on American Republics Affairs, *Survey of the Alliance for Progress*, 91st Cong., 1st sess., Doc. No. 91-17, April 29, 1969 (Washington: U.S. Government Printing Office, 1969), p. 586.

20. See Joseph Page, *The Revolution That Never Was: Northeast Brazil 1955–1964* (New York: Grossman Publishers, 1972), p. 232.

21. Philip Siekman, "When Executives Turned Revolutionaries," *Fortune*, September 1964, p. 214.

22. Quoted in Skidmore, p. 326.

23. Quoted in E. Bradford Burns, *Nationalism in Brazil* (New York: Frederick A. Praeger, 1968), pp. 115–116.

24. Quoted in Peter D. Bell, p. 90.

25. Ibid.

26. David E. Bell, Administrator, AID, April 20, 1964. U.S.,

Congress, House, Subcommittee of the Committee on Appropriations, *Foreign Operations Appropriations for 1965, Part 2*, 88th Cong., 2nd sess., (Washington: U.S. Government Printing Office, 1964), p. 193.

27. *Department of State Bulletin*, April 20, 1964, p. 609; also see Tad Szulc, "Washington Sends 'Warmest' Wishes to Brazil's Leaders," *New York Times*, April 3, 1964, p. 1.

28. *Congressional Record—Senate*, April 3, 1964, pp. 6851–6852.

29. Quoted in Joseph Page, p. 217.

30. U.S., Congress, Senate, Committee on Foreign Relations, *Nomination of Lincoln Gordon to be Assistant Secretary of State for Inter-American Affairs*, 89th Cong., 2nd sess., February 7, 1966 (Washington: U.S. Government Printing Office, 1966), p. 11.

31. Stuart H. Van Dyke, Director of USAID mission to Brazil, February 9, 1968. U.S., Congress, House, Subcommittee of the Committee on Government Operations, *U.S. Aid Operations in Latin America Under the Alliance for Progress*, 90th Cong., 2nd sess., January 24, 25, 27, 29, February 1, 2, 4, 6, 8, 9, 12, 13, and 15, 1968 (Washington: U.S. Government Printing Office, 1969), p. 496.

32. "Business Confidence Returns to Brazil: Castelo Branco Draws a Bead on Balanced Budget," *Business International*, May 29, 1964, p. 1; "The Long Tricky Path Facing Brazil," *Business Week*, April 11, 1964, p. 72.

33. "How Corporations are Adapting Operations to the Improved Investment Climate in Brazil," *Business International*, December 24, 1965, p. 410.

34. Economist Intelligence Unit, *Quarterly Economic Review of Brazil*, no. 55, August 1965, p. 4.

35. Ibid., p. 9.

36. Peter D. Bell, p. 95.

37. "U.S. Grants $50 Million Loan," *New York Times*, June 25, 1964, p. 8.

38. Economist Intelligence Unit, *Quarterly Economic Review of Brazil*, no. 50, August 1964, p. 3; "Brazil is Allowed More Time to Pay its Debts to 10 Creditor Nations," *Wall Street Journal*, July 3, 1964, p. 16.

39. "U.S. to Grant Brazil $375 Million of Aid in Economic Projects, Food Sales and Loan," *Wall Street Journal*, December 14, 1964, p. 28; Juan de Onis, "U.S. Gives Brazil a Billion in Aid," *New York Times*, December 15, 1964, p. 11.

40. Stephen Girard, President of Kaiser Jeep Corporation, following his corporation's decision to invest $32 million in expansion activities in Brazil. Quoted in Ed Cony, "Back in Brazil: Some U.S. Firms Begin Increasing Investments in Latin Land Again," *Wall Street Journal*, October 7, 1964, p. 11.

41. Eric N. Bablanoff, "Brazilian Development and the International Economy," in Joan Saunders, ed., *Modern Brazil: New Patterns and Development* (Gainesville: University of Florida Press, 1971), p. 205.

42. Ibid., p. 209.

43. Business International Corporation, *Brazil: New Business Power in Latin America* (New York: May 1971), p. 75; *Business Latin America*, April 3, 1969, p. 111.

44. "Brazil: Some Success, Much to Do," *Business Week*, January 22, 1966, p. 62.

45. U.S. Agency for International Development, *U.S. Overseas Loans and Grants and Assistance from International Organizations*, July 1, 1945–June 30, 1971, May 1972, as quoted in *NACLA's Latin America and Empire Report* ("Brazil: Development for Whom"), April 1973, p. 16; U.S. Agency for International Development, *U.S. Overseas Assistance and Grants and Assistance from International Organizations*, July 1, 1945–June 30, 1973, p. 40.

46. U.S., Congress, House, Committee on Foreign Affairs, *Report of the Special Study Mission to the Dominican Republic, Guyana, Brazil and Paraguay*, 90th Cong., 1st sess., Committee Print, April 27, 1967 (Washington: U.S. Government Printing Office, 1967;, pp. 45–46.

47. Airgram from AID Brazil, dated January 13, 1967, as quoted in ibid., p. 42.

48. U.S. General Accounting Office, *U.S. Foreign Aid to Education: Does Brazil Need It?*, Report to the Congress by the Comptroller General of the United States, Washington, D.C., B-133283, July 30, 1973, p. 21.

49. Ibid., pp. 34, 40.
50. U.S., Congress, House, *U.S. Aid Operations in Latin America under the Alliance for Progress*, p. 549.
51. U.S., Congress, Senate, *United States Policies and Programs in Brazil*, pp. 165–166.
52. U.S. General Accounting Office, *U.S. Foreign Aid to Education: Does Brazil Need It?*, p. 17.
53. In 1967, for example, AID held up disbursements to Brazil when the junta began to ease credit and wage controls to combat a recessionary trend in the economy, and only resumed disbursing credits when the stabilization measures were reapplied. In late 1968, $188 million in AID loan authorizations were placed "under review" and the suspension was not lifted until May 1969. See Peter D. Bell, pp. 588–589, 597.
54. U.S. Agency for International Development, *U.S. Overseas Loans and Grants and Assistance from International Organizations*, July 1, 1945–June 30, 1973, p. 40.
55. Interview No. 3–2, World Bank, Washington, D.C., June 6, 1974; Interview No. 3–7, Inter-American Development Bank, Washington, D.C., June 12, 1974.
56. U.S. Agency for International Development, *U.S. Overseas Loans and Grants and Assistance from International Organizations*, July 1, 1945—June 30 1973, p. 182. During the first half of 1974, the World Bank's enthusiasm for Brazilian development projects continued unabated. In June, it approved a $36 million loan for a water supply and sewage project in Minas Gerias and a $81 million loan for a hydroelectric power scheme to serve a large part of northeast Brazil. In the previous month, the World Bank's private enterprise affiliate, the International Finance Corporation (IFC) supported by financial institutions in the U.S. and Europe, made a $64.5 million investment in the Brazilian steel industry. See International Bank for Reconstruction and Development, *Bank Press Release*, no. 74/44, June 6, 1974 and no. 74/45, June 6, 1974; International Finance Corporation, *Press Release*, no. 74/9, May 8, 1974.
57. "Brazilian Government-Owned Company Forging New International Links," *Business Latin America*, May 8, 1969, p. 150.

58. Economist Intelligence Unit, *Quarterly Economic Review of Brazil*, no. 1, January 1970, p. 11; no. 1, January 1973, p. 4; no. 1, February 1974, p. 5; Jose Serra, "The Brazilian 'Economic Miracle'," in James Petras, ed., p. 104.

59. "Major Brazilian Firms Boost Profits in Wave of Economic Euphoria," *Business Latin America*, September 24, 1970, p. 308; "Brazilian Firms Boost Profits in 1970 But May Feel Squeezed Next Year," *Business Latin America*, September 23, 1971, p. 302.

60. "U.S. Companies in Latin America Invest More But Earn Less in 1970," *Business Latin America*, December 2, 1971, p. 377.

61. Quoted in *The Nation*, December 20, 1971, p. 645.

62. Economist Intelligence Unit, *Quarterly Economic Review of Brazil*, no. 3, July 1972, p. 15; no. 3, August 1973, p. 16.

63. U.S. Department of Commerce, Bureau of International Commerce, *Foreign Economic Trends—Brazil*, March 27, 1973, p. 9.

64. "Profitability in Brazil Looms High as Companies Continue to Cash in on Boom," *Business Latin America*, December 7, 1972, p. 385; "Firms Reap Impressive Profits From Brazil's Economic Boom," *Business Latin America*, March 6, 1974, p. 76.

65. "Profitability in Brazil Looms High as Companies Continue to Cash in on Boom," p. 385.

66. "Geisal Administration in Brazil Maps Out Economic Plans," *Business Latin America*, March 27, 1974, p. 97.

67. "Brazil Continues to Attract Major Foreign Investment," *Business Latin America*, April 10, 1974, p. 113.

68. "Latin America's Fast Growth," *Business Week*, July 6, 1974, p. 107.

69. "Brazil Continues to Attract Major Foreign Investment," p. 113.

70. Interview No. 3–6, U.S. Department of Defense, Virginia, June 10, 1974.

71. U.S., Congress, Senate, Subcommittee of the Committee on Appropriations, *Foreign Assistance and Related Programs Appropriations for Fiscal Year 1972*, 92nd Cong., 1st sess.,

1971 (Washington: U.S. Government Printing Office, 1971), pp. 742–743.

72. U.S., Congress, House, Committee on Foreign Affairs, Subcommittee on National Security Policy and Scientific Development, *Report of the Special Study Mission to Latin America on I. Military Assistance Training; II. Developmental Television*, 91st Cong., Committee Print, May 7, 1970 (Washington: U.S. Government Printing Office, 1970), p. 6.

73. Ibid., p. 5.

74. Interview No. 3–6.

75. Interview No. 2–16. In an analysis of the fishing agreement signed between the United States and Brazil in September 1972, Senator Clayborne Pell perceptively observed that the "compact without addressing the controversial sovereignty question, is primarily designed to forestall any confrontation before the 1973 International Law of the Sea Conference. Its provisions completely avoid the disputed issue concerning Brazil's 200-mile territorial sea and are written solely in terms of conservation." See Senator Pell, *Agreement with Brazil Concerning Shrimp*, Executive Rept. 92-37, U.S., Congress, Senate, 92nd Cong., 2nd sess., October 2, 1972, p. 2; U.S., Congress, Senate, Committee on Foreign Relations, Subcommittee on Oceans and International Environment, *Shrimp Agreement with Brazil*, 92nd Cong., 2nd sess. September 28, 1972 (Washington: U.S. Government Printing Office, 1972).

76. U.S., Congress, House, Committee on Foreign Affairs, Subcommittee on Inter-American Affairs, *New Directions for the 1970's—Part 2: Development Assistance Options for Latin America*, 92nd Cong., 1st Sess., February 18, July 12, 19, 26, 27, and August 4, 1971 (Washington: U.S. Government Printing Office, 1971), p. 265. Regarding the overall relationship, a State Department official responded similarly: "I would think that we are, right now, at a high point of relations between the U.S. and Brazil. At a high plateau of excellent relations that I don't believe it is possible to get any better." Interview No. 2–1, U.S. Department of State, Washington, D.C., June 19, 1973.

77. Interview No. 2–3: U.S. Department of State, Washington, D.C., June 11, 1973.

78. Interview No. 2–1: U.S. Department of State, June 19, 1973.

79. Interview No. 2–16.

80. Charles A. Meyer, Assistant Secretary of State for Inter-American Affairs, U.S., Congress, Senate, Committee on Foreign Relations, Subcommittee on Western Hemisphere Affairs, *United States Relations with Peru*, 91st Cong., 1st sess., April 14, 16 and 17, 1969 (Washington: U.S. Government Printing Office, 1969), p. 117.

81. Ernst and Ernst, *A National Profile—Peru*, International Business Series, New York, February 1974, p. 19.

82. U.S., Congress, House, Committee on Banking and Currency, Subcommittee on International Finance, *To Authorize the United States to Provide Additional Financial Resources to the Asian Development Bank and the Inter-American Development Bank*, 92nd Cong., 1st sess. October 26, 1971 (Washington: U.S. Government Printing Office, 1971), p. 139. See also Murray Rossant, "The Big Stick is Now Economic," *New York Times*, October 10, 1971, p. E8.

83. Interview No. 2–16.

84. Richard W. Dye, "Peru, the United States, and Hemisphere Relations," *Inter-American Economic Affairs*, Autumn 1972, p. 73.

85. Quoted in Mark L. Chadwin, "Foreign Policy Report: Nixon Administration Debates New Position Paper on Latin America," *National Journal*, January 15, 1972, p. 103.

86. Lewis Diuguid, "U. S. Relaxes Policy on Loans to Peru," *Washington Post*, September 20, 1973, p. A21.

87. International Bank for Reconstruction and Development (World Bank), *The Current Economic Position and Prospects of Peru* (Washington, D.C.: December 1973) pp. 17–18. This report was based on the findings of an economic mission which visited Peru in November and December 1972 and in January 1973.

88. Chadwin, p. 103.

89. Interview No. 2–21, U.S. Department of State, Washington, D.C., August 21, 1973.

90. Interview No. 2–16.

91. U.S., Congress, House, Committee on Appropriations, Sub-committee on Foreign Operations and Related Agencies, *Foreign Assistance and Related Agencies Appropriations for 1974, Part 1,* 93rd Cong., 1st sess. (Washington: U.S. Government Printing Office, 1973), p. 1116.

92. Quoted in "Secretary Rogers' Latin America Tour Brings No Concrete Changes in Policy," *Business Latin America,* June 7, 1973, p. 179. "We don't oppose foreign investment," declared Peruvian Foreign Minister Miguel de la Flor, in commenting on the oil contracts awarded to U.S. companies. "We want it and we need it. But we don't want it to occur the way it did prior to 1968, when it led to Peru's political and economic dependency." Quoted in John P. Wallach, "Dispute Over Copper Mines Perils U.S.-Peru Relations," *Washington Post,* August 16, 1973, p. G13.

93. "Secretary Rogers' Latin America Tour Brings No Concrete Changes in Policy," p. 179; Diuguid, p. A21; "Peru: High Stakes," *Latin America,* September 14, 1973, p. 295; International Bank for Reconstruction and Development, *Bank Press Release,* no. 73/63, August 17, 1973; U.S., Congress, House, Committee on Banking and Currency, Subcommittee on International Finance, *Providing for Additional U.S. Contributions to the Asian Development Bank and the International Development Association,* 93rd Cong., 1st sess., November 14; December 3 and 6, 1973 (Washington: U.S. Government Printing Office, 1973), p. 17.

94. "U.S. Envoy's Talks to Peru Hint at Change in Mood," *Business Latin America,* August 30, 1973, p. 277.

95. Interview No. 3–10, World Bank, Washington, D.C., June 13, 1974.

96. Interview No. 3–2.

97. See "Peru's Expropriation of Cerro Has Few Repercussions," *Business Latin America,* January 16, 1974, pp. 19–20; "Cerro Unit Nationalized by Peru: Compensation Talks are Progressing," *Wall Street Journal,* January 2, 1974, p. 4. On the Greene appointment, see Richard Lawrence, "World Bank Approves Loan to Peru," *Journal of Commerce,* August 15, 1973, p. 1.

Manufacturers Hanover, at the time, was in the process of preparing to lead a consortium of U.S. banks in lending Peru $130 million in credits. See "Peru: High Stakes," p. 295. The willingness of U.S. private banks to reopen the lines of credit to Peru was first evidenced in April, when Wells Fargo Bank of California made arrangements for a $130 million loan to the military government. A U.S. banker resident in Peru at the time explained the decision to invest: "Frankly, we feel Peru is a very good risk. . . . This is a stable government—whether it's left leaning or not. There are no riots in the streets, and there is a relatively strong currency." Quoted in Jonathan Kandell, "U.S. Aid Embargo Straining Peru Ties," *New York Times*, April 18, 1973, p. 8.

98. Stephen Morrow, "U.S., Peru Agreement Seen Near," *Washington Post*, February 8, 1974, p. A17; H. J. Maidenberg, "Peru Will Pay $76 Million for Seized U.S. Concerns," *New York Times*, February 20, 1974, p. 4; "U.S. Settles Feud on Eleven Firms Peru Nationalized," *Wall Street Journal*, February 20, 1974, p. 4.

99. "U.S.-Peru Compensation Deal Settles Expropriation Claims," *Business Latin America*, February 27, 1974, p. 67.

100. Stephen Klaidman, "Peru-U.S. Scars are Healing," *Washington Post*, December 26, 1973, p. A16.

101. Interview No. 2–18.

Nevertheless, some policy-makers within the Department of Defense continue to express concern over certain aspects of the Peruvian military junta's policies, such as their purchase of Soviet military equipment:

> The military government in Peru, as revolutionary military government, is at best left-of-center and, I must say, going further to the left. (Interview No. 3–6)

102. Interview No. 2–16.

103. Interview No. 3–3.

104. The 1964 Brazilian military coup was an important point of reference for the Chilean Right and other opponents of the Allende government. Brazilian business and private groups

who played critical roles in the overthrow of the Goulart government in 1964 were, in fact, actively involved in channeling thousands of dollars and considerable quantities of arms to anti-Allende organizations in Chile as well as in the training of Chilean rightists in the politics of coup-making. The Brazilians were instrumental in getting the Chilean Right and the Christian Democratic Party to set up political think tanks to coordinate antigovernment strategy (a successful tactic in the Brazilian case). The Brazilians also pointed out to their Chilean counterparts that the manipulation of women in support of the coup strategy was essential: "We ourselves created a large and successful women's movement, and Campaign for Women, and Chile copied it." It was a crucial factor, the Brazilians emphasized, in giving the military the impression "that they have wide civilian support." For a detailed analysis of the Brazilian involvement, see Marlisle Simons, "The Brazilian Connection," *Washington Post*, January 6, 1974, p. B8.

5. *Foreign Economic Policy, the Copper Conflict, and the Foreign Debt*

1. Interview No. 2–18.
2. Quoted in Szulc, "The View from Langley," p. C5.
3. Interviews with various U.S. policy-makers.
4. Quoted in Jack Anderson, "ITT Hope of Ousting Allende Remote," *Washington Post*, March 28, 1972, p. B11 and "A Hint Not Taken: Nixon Avoids Allende," *Washington Post*, December 10, 1972, p. C7.
5. Interview No. 2–20, Council on International Economic Policy, Washington, D.C., August 20, 1973.
6. Interview No. 2–18.

Another U.S. policy-maker assessed the interdepartmental positions in retrospect:

> Policy-making on Chile was done on a consensus basis. I don't think that hardline/softline is a fair characteriza-

tion of the Chilean situation because my impression is that there was a pretty strong basis of agreement within the U.S. government that this was an appropriate policy in respect of Chile. I don't have the impression that there were any significant interagency battles over harder or more moderate posture vis-à-vis Chile. (Interview No. 3–3)

7. Quoted in Dom Bonafede, "White House Report: Peterson Unit Helps Shape Tough International Economic Policy," *National Journal*, October 13, 1971, p. 2241.

8. Ibid., p. 2238.

9. U.S., Congress, House, Committee on Banking and Currency, Subcommittee on International Trade, *To Establish a Council on International Economic Policy*, 92nd Cong., 2nd sess., May 31, 1972 (Washington: U.S. Government Printing Office, 1972), p. 3.

10. Peter G. Peterson, *The United States in the Changing World Economy* (Washington: U.S. Government Printing Office, 1971), Vol. 1: *A Foreign Economic Perspective*, p. 51.

11. Quoted in Bonafede, p. 2239.

12. Frank V. Fowlkes, "Economic Report: Connally Revitalizes Treasury Assumes Stewardship of Nixon's New Economic Policy," *National Journal*, October 2, 1971, p. 1990.

13. Chadwin, p. 106.

14. Quoted in Michael C. Jensen, "U.S. Reportedly Withheld Ecuador Aid on I.T.T. Plea," *New York Times*, August 10, 1973, p. 37. Also see, "When $25,000 stood between ITT and Ecuador," *Business Week*, August 11, 1973, pp. 102–103.

15. Dan Morgan, "Officials Say Aid to Ecuador Halted as ITT Bargained," *Washington Post*, August 10, 1973, p. A2.

16. U.S., Congress, House, Committee on Banking and Currency, Subcommittee on International Finance, *To Provide for Increased Participation by the United States in the International Development Association*, 92nd Cong., 1st sess., July 6, 1971 (Washington: U.S. Government Printing Office, 1971), p. 94.

17. Under-Secretary of the Treasury Charles E. Walker, in a letter

to House Inter-American Affairs Subcommittee Chairman Fascell, as quoted in U.S., Congress, House, *New Directions for the 1970s, Part 2: Development Assistance Options for Latin America*, p. 116.

18. U.S., Congress, House, *To Provide for Increased Participation by the United States in the International Development Association*, p. 101.

19. Interview No. 2–17, U.S. Department of the Treasury, Washington, D.C., August 13, 1973.

20. U.S., Congress, House, *New Directions for the 1970s, Part 2: Development Assistance Options for Latin America*, pp. 113–118. The U.S. government controls approximately one-quarter of the votes on the World Bank board, giving it a virtual veto power over loan decisions, especially when one considers that "other major shareholders such as West Germany are very anxious to avoid offending it." See "Chile: War of Nerves," *Latin America*, October 20, 1972, p. 335.

21. Quoted in "Connally's Hard Sell against Inflation," *Business Week*, July 10, 1971, p. 65.

22. Both Allende and the Chilean congress deemed "unacceptable" Kennecott and Anaconda's bigger profits from their Chilean operations as compared to their other operations around the world. See John Strasma, "Some Economic Aspects of Non-Violent Revolution in Chile and Peru, with Emphasis on the Mining and Manufacturing Sectors" (Paper presented to the Latin American Studies Association Convention, Austin, Texas, December 1971), p. 17. A decision on the other U.S. copper corporation, Cerro, was held in abeyance.

23. Quoted in Benjamin Welles, "Chile's Move Spurs U.S. to 'Get Tough,'" *New York Times*, September 30, 1971, p. 3.

24. Quoted in "U.S. Expects 'Adequate' Chilean Payment for Nationalized Mines," *Wall Street Journal*, September 30, 1971, p. 10.

25. "U.S. Responds to Chilean Decision on Compensation for Expropriation," *Department of State Bulletin*, November 1, 1971, p. 478. When the Allende government started moving against U.S. interests, it did so as part of a general offensive

against private Chilean interests. Copper, however, was an isolated sector, not interlocked with substantial Chilean interests. This explains the incapacity of the United States to mobilize internal groups within Chile in support of its position. In response to the Rogers statement, the Chilean opposition parties publicly declared their full support of the government's action. "In matters where the national interest is at stake," declared the president of the Christian Democratic Party, "there is no distinction between the Government and Opposition." Quoted in Juan de Onis, "Rogers' Stand Spurs Unity Drive in Chile," *New York Times*, October 15, 1971, p. 3.

26. U.S., Congress, House, Committee on Foreign Affairs, Subcommittee on Inter-American Affairs, *Recent Developments in Chile*, 92nd Cong., 1st sess., October 15, 1971 (Washington: U.S. Government Printing Office, 1971), pp. 3–4. An NSC staff member agreed that the payments demanded "would have hurt the Chilean economy. No doubt about it." Interview No. 2–18, National Security Council, Washington, D.C., August 14, 1973.

27. Interview No. 2–15, U.S. Department of State, Washington, D.C., July 10, 1973.

28. "Chile-U.S. Clash Over Copper Poses New Threat to Hemisphere," *Business Latin America*, October 7, 1971, pp. 313–314.

29. "Six Concerns Embroiled in Seizure by Chile Are Called in by Rogers," *Wall Street Journal*, October 25, 1971, p. 10; Jeremiah O'Leary, "U.S. May Halt Aid to Chile in Copper Seizure Action," *Washington Star*, October 22, 1971, p. A1; Benjamin Welles, "Rogers Threatens Chilean Aid Cutoff in Expropriation," *New York Times*, October 23, 1971, p. 1.

30. U.S., Congress, Senate, *Multinational Corporations and United States Foreign Policy, Part 2*, pp. 975–979.

31. North American Congress on Latin America (NACLA), *New Chile*, p. 42. According to an ITT memorandum, Anaconda had also gotten Senator Mansfield to "assist them in attempting to press for a favorable tax ruling from IRS to take the Chilean loss as an ordinary loss rather than a capital loss." U.S.,

Congress, Senate, *Multinational Corporations and United States Foreign Policy, Part 2*, p. 954.

32. Ibid., p. 940.

33. Ibid., p. 971.

34. U.S., Congress, Senate, *Multinational Corporations and United States Foreign Policy, Part 1*, pp. 328–329. U.S. public policy linked Chile's creditworthiness to three main criteria: the Allende government's management of the economy, its attitude toward international debt obligations, and its position on the interrelated questions of expropriation and compensation. In practice, however, the notion of creditworthiness has been used to distinguish between political regimes: to contrast them in terms of the kinds of policies adopted toward critical political groups in the society, and as regards their external policies. The severe repression of the masses by the military government in Brazil since 1964, together with the junta's anticommunism and receptivity to foreign investment, contrasted favorably with the national-popular policies of the Goulart period. As a result, U.S. and international lines of credit increased dramatically. The Peruvian military junta's creditworthiness was in part based on its margination of the masses from any effective role in the society. The U.S. government granted $35,573,000 in aid to the right-wing government of Hugo Banzer in Bolivia, which ousted the leftist government of General Torres in August 1971, "even though the economy was in a shambles." In testimony before a House subcommittee, Herman Kleine, Deputy Coordinator for the Alliance for Progress, gave as one of the reasons for this aid the fact that the conservative counterrevolution had "improved [the] climate for foreign investment. . . ." See Laurence Stern, "Aid Used As Choke on Allende," *Washington Post,* September 19, 1973, p. A14; U.S., Congress, House, Committee on Appropriations, Subcommittee on Foreign Operations and Related Agencies, *Foreign Assistance and Related Appropriations for 1973, Part 1*, 92nd Cong., 1st sess. (Washington: U.S. Government Printing Office, 1972), p. 1091.

35. *NACLA's Latin America and Empire Report*, January 1973, p.

15. "The bankers and exporters interviewed were quick to deny any direct, political pressure to cease giving credits to Chile. However, relations between the Treasury Department and the New York banks are on a day-to-day, personal basis and one banker did admit: 'We are influenced to a considerable degree by the attitude of the U.S. government—it couldn't be otherwise. We deal with the USSR, with Yugoslavia and China, but not with Chile. Why? Because of the policy of the government.' " Ibid., p. 16.

36. *Facts on File*, August 12–18, 1971, p. 640. In October 1970, when it was clear that Allende would be confirmed as president by the Chilean congress, the Export-Import Bank immediately reclassified Chile's credit standing from a C to a D—the poor risks category. See Economist Intelligence Unit, *Quarterly Economic Review of Chile*, no. 4, December 1970, p. 5.

37. Stern, "Aid Used As Choke on Allende," p. A14.

38. Marilyn Berger, "Chile Seeks to Acquire Jets," *Washington Post*, June 4, 1971, p. A10. Also see testimony of John H. Crimmins, Acting Assistant Secretary of State, before the Senate Foreign Relations Committee. Crimmins attempted to justify the bank decision while, at the same time, supporting an increase in U.S. military credits to Chile. Committee Chairman William Fulbright pointed to the contradictory nature of Crimmins' position:

> I can only emphasize it seems to me a very ironic thing that you even question the sale of a 707 and yet you positively already recommended an increase in military sales. It seems a very odd posture for the United States to be in of even having doubts about giving Chile the right to buy on the usual terms, with the Export Bank which was established for that purpose, a civilian transport which I am sure Boeing is most anxious to sell, and then without any hesitation apparently recommending a $6 million increase in the military sales. This just seems utterly inconsistent to what I thought was our policy.

U.S., Congress, Senate, Committee on Foreign Relations,

Inter-American Development Bank Funds for Special Operations, 92nd Cong., 1st sess., June 4, 1971 (Washington, D.C.: U.S. Government Printing Office, 1971), p. 59. The *Washington Post* called the episode "a major failure of American policy," and declared that "no self-respecting government, Marxist or otherwise, can be expected to dance a jig for Henry Kearns." Senator Kennedy called it a "heavy-handed" policy. See "Bullying Chile," *Washington Post,* September 14, 1971, p. A18, Kennedy, pp. 2–3.

39. "Chile: The Jet Set," *Latin America,* August 20, 1971, p. 265.
40. Tad Szulc, "U.S. Retaliating for Foreign Seizures," *New York Times,* August 14, 1971, p. 3. One White House aide said of the State Department that it "always tries for a position of perpetual flexibility." Quoted in Chadwin, p. 97.
41. Stern, "Aid Used as Choke on Allende," p. A14.
42. Interview No. 3–8, Inter-American Committee on the Alliance for Progress, Washington, D.C., June 12, 1974.
43. Stern, "Aid Used as Choke on Allende," p. A14.
44. Quoted in International Bank for Reconstruction and Development, International Finance Corporations, Annual Meetings of the Board of Governors, September 25–29, 1972, *Summary Proceedings* (Washington: International Development Association, 1972) pp. 58–59.
45. Interview No. 3–2. The general consensus within the bank was that "the day-to-day operations [of the Chilean economy] were not affected by the fall in short-term credits," and that the overall decline in all categories of loans and credits to Allende's Chile "made no difference at all" or only "had a marginal impact" on the process of gradual economic deterioration. See Interview No. 3–10, and Interview No. 3–2.

    The Russians did provide large-scale long-term credits while the World Bank's policies had less to do with the "investment-savings rate" and more to do with Washington's concern with the rate of expropriation of U.S. business and growth of workers' power.

46. U.S., Congress, House, *To Authorize the United States to Provide Additional Financial Resources to the Asian Develop-*

ment Bank and the Inter-American Development Bank, p. 139. Also see Murray Rossant, "The Big Stick is Now Economic," p. E8.

Although U.S. nationals comprise only 18 percent of the total staff of the Inter-American Development Bank and approximately 27 percent of the total staff of the World Bank/International Development Association, in both institutions U.S. officials occupy about 42 percent of the top management positions. See U.S., Congress, House, Committee on Foreign Affairs, *The United States and the Multilateral Development Banks*, 93rd Cong., 2nd sess., March 1974 (Washington: U.S. Government Printing Office, 1974), pp. 214–215.

47. Teresa Hayter, *Aid as Imperialism* (Harmonsworth: Pelican Books, 1971), p. 44.

48. Lewis H. Diuguid, "Schweitzer Gains Backers for IMF in Latin America," *Washington Post*, October 29, 1972, p. F1.

49. Sigmund, p. 329. By January 1973, the Allende government had drawn $187.8 million in credits from the IMF. See "Chile Receives SDR Credit From IMF to Alleviate Country's Payments Problem," *Business Latin America*, January 25, 1973, p. 31.

50. OAS, Inter-American Social and Economic Council, Inter-American Committee on the Alliance for Progress, p. 12.

51. Ibid., p. 148.

52. Ibid., p. 139. The volume of copper production and exports in 1971 was higher than in any year since 1961, but the value of exports declined by 16.2 percent in relation to 1970 because of a 20.6 percent decline in the price of copper. See ibid., p. 10.

53. Economist Intelligence Unit, *Quarterly Economic Review of Chile*, no. 2, May 1973, p. 22.

54. Economist Intelligence Unit, *Quarterly Economic Review of Chile*, no. 3, September 1973, pp. 23–24. On the drop in foreign exchange reserves, this source reported in September 1972 that reserves had declined from almost $300 million to around $40 million within the space of just over a year. See Economist Intelligence Unit, *Quarterly Economic Review of Chile*, no. 3, September 1972, p. 10.

55. Economist Intelligence Unit, *Quarterly Economic Review of Chile*, no. 3, September 1973, pp. 23–24.

56. U.S., Congress, House, Committee on Foreign Affairs, Subcommittee on Foreign Economic Policy, *New Realities and New Directions in United States Foreign Economic Policy*, 92nd Cong., 1st sess., February 28, 1972 (Washington: U.S. Government Printing Office, 1972), p. 21. On the Treasury position, also see Benjamin Welles, "We Don't Have Any Friends Anyway," *New York Times*, August 15, 1971, p. E6; Benjamin Welles, "U.S. Weighs Policy on Expropriation," *New York Times*, August 22, 1971, p. 11.

57. "President Nixon Issues Policy Statement on Economic Assistance and Investment Security in Developing Nations," *Department of State Bulletin*, February 7, 1972, pp. 153–154. Also see Richard Nixon, *U.S. Foreign Policy for the 1970s*, A Report to the Congress, February 9, 1972 (Washington: U.S. Government Printing Office, 1972), pp. 990–991.

58. Interview No. 2–19. This official also thought that "the Cuban experience [in the early 1960s] had quite a bit of impact; something that filtered down. Treasury was going to make sure that U.S. investors would be protected if expropriations took place."

A former policy advisor with the National Security Council was more critical of this tactic as it affected long-term U.S. economic interests in Latin America:

> The 1972 approach places great emphasis upon the issue of compensation. In fact, the position is that no expropriation is legal, but negative, and something which affects our aid policy and our actions in the international agencies. This is a short-sighted point of view. We have significant interests that go beyond investment interests. . . . This type of policy may be creating harm. It is more important to view this in a broader context. Antagonistic response being applied in cases of expropriation reinforces attitudes, and therefore affects attitudes on a whole range of other issues important to the United States. (Interview No. 2–16)

59. Interview No. 2–21.

60. Interview No. 2–17. The president established a special inter-departmental "expropriations" committee, chaired by the assistant secretary of state for economic affairs. See National Advisory Council on International Monetary and Financial Policies, *Annual Report*, July 1, 1971–June 30, 1972, to the president and to Congress, December 8, 1972 (Washington, D.C.: U.S. Department of the Treasury, December 1972), p. 35.

61. Quoted in "U.S. Policy on Foreign Seizure of Assets Stiffened; Bilateral and Other Aid Curbed," *Wall Street Journal*, January 20, 1972, p. 5.

62. "The Nixon Warning on Expropriation: What It Will Mean to Companies," *Business Latin America*, January 27, 1972, p. 26.

63. Ibid.

64. Interview No. 2–16.

65. U.S., Congress, Senate, Committee on Foreign Relations; House, Committee on Foreign Affairs, *Legislation on Foreign Relations*, Joint Committee Print, March 1973 (Washington: U.S. Government Printing Office, 1973), pp. 990–991.

66. Interview No. 2–19. In September 1972, the U.S. General Accounting Office made available for publication the unclassified sections of its report on the "U.S. System for Appraising and Evaluating Inter-American Development Bank Projects and Activities," dated August 22, 1972. In a section of the report entitled "Loans to Countries Involved in Expropriation of Property," the GAO was apparently highly critical of Treasury policy within IDB. This can be inferred, not from this section of the report, which was heavily censored, but from the Treasury Department's response to the still classified sections of the report.

> An implicit hard-line, high profile approach, involving not only a rigid posture in Inter-American negotiations but also in aggressive, confrontational U.S. posture in the working decisions of the Bank underlies this section. In the best judgement of the Treasury it is wrong to equate effective U.S. management with this approach. . . .

See U.S., Congress, House, Committee on Foreign Affairs, Subcommittee on Inter-American Affairs, *Treasury Department Management of U.S. Participation in the Inter-American Development Bank*, 92nd Cong., 2nd sess. (Appendix), September 21, 1972 (Washington: U.S. Government Printing Office, 1972), p. 44.

67. Quoted in International Bank for Reconstruction and Development, International Finance Corporation, International Development Association, *Summary Proceedings*, 1973 Annual Meeting of the Board of Governors, Nairobi, Kenya, September 24–28, 1973 (Washington), p. 193.

68. U.S., Congress, House, *To Provide for Additional U.S. Contributions to the Asian Development Bank and the International Development Association*, p. 35.

69. U.S., Congress, House, *The United States and the Multilateral Development Banks*, pp. 112–114. In noting that, "for the most part, the banks have channeled funds to countries in which the United States has strategic and diplomatic interests and have refrained from lending to countries with which the United States has had investment disputes" (p. 5), the study concluded on the following note:

> Participation in the banks serves two general foreign policy interests of the United States. First, the banks assist in pursuit of general goals involving the structure of international affairs and the prestige and influence of the United States. Second, they serve as vehicles for assisting countries favored by the United States and for influencing economic affairs of countries with which the U.S. Government has international disagreements. (p. 131)

70. Norman Girvan, *Copper in Chile* (Mona, Jamaica: University of the West Indies, Institute of Social and Economic Research, 1972), p. 59.

71. Keith Griffin, *Underdevelopment in Spanish America* (London: George Allen and Unwin, 1971), p. 152.

72. According to Anaconda Vice-Chairman William E. Quigley, "in February 1969, Frei informed Anaconda that as the

political situation was developing he was unable to control those elements advocating expropriation. In May Frei said that unless there was renegotiation with Anaconda he would be bound to support an expropriation bill. Mr. Quigley said that at this point he went to Chile and negotiated night and day until June 26." See NACLA's *Latin America and Empire Report*, p. 25.

73. Girvan, p. 61.
74. James D. Cockcroft, Henry Frundt, Dale L. Johnson, and the Chile Rutgers Research Group, "I.T.T., Multinationals, and Chile" (Unpublished paper, Rutgers University, 1972), p. 10.
75. OAS, Inter-American Economic and Social Council, Inter-American Committee on the Alliance for Progress, p. 127.
76. Griffin, pp. 172, 164.
77. Chile Research Group, Rutgers University, "Chile Nationalization of Copper," in Dale L. Johnson, ed., *The Chilean Road to Socialism* (New York: Doubleday Anchor, 1973), p. 28.
78. Girvan, p. 60.
79. Chile Research Group, p. 28.
80. Girvan, p. 60.
81. Address by Carlos Fortin, official of the Chilean Government Copper Corporation (CODELCO), before the American Bar Association, New York, reprinted in CORFO, *Chile Economic News*, June 1, 1973, p. 19. Some idea of the continuing high rate of profit during the Chileanization period may be gleaned from the following figures: the rate of return on all U.S. investments in the Chilean copper industry in 1967 was 27 percent. In 1968 it was 26 percent. The figure for Anaconda in 1969 was 39.5 percent, while for Kennecott it was 24.1 percent. See Chile Research Group, p. 28.
82. See Juan de Onis, "U.S. Warns Chile Her Plan to Take Over Copper Holdings Could Hurt Relations," *New York Times*, February 1971, p. 2. Although a new U.S. ambassador to Chile was appointed in April, some months elapsed before the withdrawal of the incumbent U.S. Ambassador Edward Korry. "The major reason appear[ed] to be the confidence that United States copper companies expressed in Mr. Korry as

spokesman before the Chilean Government on United States views." Juan de Onis, "U.S. Chilean Relations Running into Serious Snags," *New York Times*, June 2, 1971, p. 13.

83. Economist Intelligence Unit, *Quarterly Economic Review of Chile*, no. 1, March 1973, p. 16 and no. 2, May 1973, p. 14. Also see, Inter-American Development Bank, *Socio-Economic Progress in Latin America*, Social Progress Trust Fund, Tenth Annual Report, February 25, 1971 (Washington: 1970), p. 150. The reversion forecast for 1973 was confirmed for January to June. The price subsequently increased to $1.0327 a pound in November, the benefits of the increase accruing to the military junta. See Economist Intelligence Unit, ibid., p. 9.

84. Quoted in *Facts on File*, October 7–13, 1971, p. 800.

85. "The Kennecott White Paper on Chile's Expropriation of the El Teniente Copper Mine," *Inter-American Economic Affairs*, Spring 1972, p. 37.

86. Quoted in Gerd Wilcke, "Kennecott to Write Off Chile Equity Investment," *New York Times*, September 8, 1972, p. 45.

87. James J. Nagle, "Kennecott Acts on Chile Copper," *New York Times*, October 5, 1972, p. 67.

88. "Chile: Facing the Blockade," *NACLA's Latin America and Empire Report*, January 1973, p. 22. Also see Gene Smith, "Copper Bedeviled by Politics," *NewYork Times*, November 5, 1972, p. F1.

89. "Freeze is Lifted on Chile Copper," *New York Times*, November 30, 1972, p. 63.

90. "West German Court Embargoes Shipment of Copper from Chile," *New York Times*, January 10, 1973, p. 51; David Binder, "Chile Criticizes Kennecott Move," *New York Times*, January 13, 1973, p. 37. According to one source, Kennecott's actions during early 1973 resulted in losses which forced CODELCO to reassign 5,000 tons of copper to alternative markets. See Economist Intelligence Unit, *Quarterly Economic Review of Chile*, no. 1, March 1970, p. 16.

91. U.S. Department of the Interior, Bureau of Mines, *Minerals Yearbook, Vol. 1, 1971* (Washington: U.S. Government Printing Office, 1973), p. 494.

92. Quoted in "Paris Court Bars Payment for Chile Copper at Kennecott's Behest, Clouding the Market," *Wall Street Journal*, October 5, 1972, p. 38. Furthermore, "Kennecott's legal offensive [had] been timed for what is known in the trade as 'the mating season' when buyers and sellers get together to make their contracts for the following year." Clyde H. Farnsworth, "Chile Assailed by Kennecott, Seeks Support," *Washington Post*, October 17, 1972, p. 55.

93. "Chile: War of Nerves," *Latin America*, October 20, 1972, p. 334.

94. Interview No. 2–18; also see Interview No. 2–21.

95. Interview No. 2–17.

96. For the complete text of Allende's speech, see the Cuban Communist Party newspaper, *Granma*, December 10, 1972, pp. 10–11.

97. Quoted in "Kennecott Declares War," *Forbes*, December 1, 1972, p. 27. An international lawyer who was consulted on the company's global strategy was more forthright: "The suits are bringing Chile to her knees . . . I predict a real purge." Quoted in ibid.

98. In December 1972, the Chilean Special Copper Tribunal ruled that Cerro Corporation should be paid $37.5 million for its nationalized mine, a figure close to the amount Cerro had claimed. Cerro's satisfactory settlement was apparently the result of three factors: it had begun operations in partnership with the Chilean government; it had not remitted any profits abroad at the time of the Anaconda and Kennecott decisions; and it had continued to supply technical help and assistance in the operation of its nationalized mine. See "Cerro: The Company That Chile Will Pay," *Business Week*, December 9, 1972, p. 30.

99. Overseas Private Investment Corporation, *Incentive Handbook—Investment Insurance* (Washington, D.C., July 1971), p. 1.

100. Marilyn Berger, "ITT Refused Chile Offer for Holdings," *Washington Post*, April 10, 1972, pp. A1, A4.

101. U.S., Congress, Senate, Committee on Foreign Relations, Subcommittee on Multinational Corporations, *Multinational*

Corporations and United States Foreign Policy, Part 3, 93rd Cong., 1st sess., July 18, 19, 20, 30, 31, August 1, 1973 (Washington: U.S. Government Printing Office, 1973), p. 141.

102. U.S., Congress, House, *The Overseas Private Investment Corporation,* p. 100.

103. From an OPIC memorandum as quoted in ibid. In respect of the copper companies, OPIC approved full payment of $11.89 million to Anaconda, and $66.9 million out of a requested $74.4 million by Kennecott. The payment to Kennecott was strongly supported by the Treasury Department and the Department of State. The latter submitted a number of "recommendations" in behalf of Kennecott. See Marcel Niedergang, "Santiago Takes a Prudent Line," *Manchester Guardian Weekly* (Le Monde Supplement), December 30, 1972, p. 25.

104. See Economist Intelligence Unit, *Quarterly Economic Review of Chile,* Annual Supplement, 1973, p. 15. The external public debt was put at $3.17 billion and the external private debt at $659,000. The estimated total debt for 1971 was approximately $3.62 billion. The World Bank figure for Chile's external public debt as of December 31, 1970, approximately $2.5 billion, seriously understates the extent of Chile's indebtedness under the Frei government. See World Bank, *Annual Report 1972,* p. 83 and World Bank Group, *Trends in Developing Countries,* 1973, Table 4.6. In March 1973, Acting Assistant Secretary of State for Inter-American Affairs John H. Crimmins estimated that the United States held 55 percent of Chile's debt to public agencies and 36 percent of the debt to private lenders. See U.S., Congress, House, *United States-Chilean Relations,* p. 4.

105. Quoted in "Chile: Its Credit Rating Is at Stake," *Business Week,* January 29, 1972, p. 37. Also see Juan de Onis, "Chile, Reserves Low, Will Seek Renegotiation of Payments on Her $3 Billion Foreign Debt," *New York Times,* November 10, 1971, p. 12; Everett G. Martin, "Chile Meets with International Creditors to Renegotiate Payments on $1.3 Billion," *Wall Street Journal,* January 10, 1972, p. 5; Juan de Onis,

"Chile, $3 Billion in Debt, Asks Creditors to Accept Moratorium on Payments," *New York Times*, January 20, 1972, p. 4.

106. Quoted in Rowland Evans and Robert Novak, "Rocky May Get State Department," *Washington Post*, February 7, 1972, p. A19.

107. Interview No. 2–15, U.S. Department of State, Washington, D.C., July 10, 1973.

108. Economist Intelligence Unit, *Quarterly Economic Review of Chile*, no. 1, March 1972, p. 5.

109. John L. Hess, "U.S. Joins in Credit Accord with Chile," *New York Times*, April 20, 1972, p. 3. The U.S. government had originally wanted the phrase "prompt, adequate, and effective" compensation accepted by the Chileans. See "Chile: Prop for Socialism," *Latin America*, April 28, 1972, p. 129.

110. U.S., Congress, House, Committee on Appropriations, Subcommittee on Foreign Operations and Related Agencies, *Foreign Assistance and Related Agencies Appropriations for 1973, Part 1*, pp. 1095–1096.

111. John Hennessy, Assistant Secretary of the Treasury for International Affairs, as quoted in U.S., Congress, Senate, Committee on Foreign Relations, Subcommittee on Multinational Corporations, *Multinational Corporations and United States Foreign Policy, Part 1*, p. 331. See also "U.S. Links Payments, Chile Talks," *Washington Post*, July 24, 1972, p. A3.

112. "Kennecott Collects on Its Insurance," *Business Week*, December 23, 1972, p. 26. Also see "U.S. and Chile Begin Talks on Rifts," *New York Times*, December 21, 1972, p. 4; Terri Shaw, "U.S.-Chile Discussions Adjourned After 3 Days," *Washington Post*, December 23, 1972, p. A16.

113. Secret testimony of CIA director, William E. Colby, and a senior official in the CIA's Office of Current Intelligence, before the House Subcommittee on Inter-American Affairs on October 11, 1973, as quoted in Szulc, "The View from Langley," p. C5.

114. Economist Intelligence Unit, *Quarterly Economic Review of Chile*, no. 2, May 1973, p. 23.

115. "Chile: Financial Confrontation," *Latin America*, April 6, 1973, pp. 105–106.
116. Interview No. 2–21. To the end, Chilean policy-makers accepted the U.S. public position without question:

> Although high-ranking members of the Allende government repeatedly alleged that large amounts of dollars were entering Chile to pay for strikes and anti-Allende campaigns, they never substantiated their claims in public. Three weeks before the coup, I raised the question of "foreign financing" in separate interviews with a senior member of the secret service and with a close aide of Allende. Both men declined to disclose any details "for policy reasons."
>
> "We are presently negotiating our debt in Washington," Allende's aide said. "These negotiations are vital to us, and we cannot afford a scandal now." (Simons, p. B3.)

6. *The United States and Militarism in Chile*

1. Michael T. Klare, *War Without End* (New York: Vintage Books, 1972), p. 280.
2. Willard F. Barber and C. Neale Ronning, *Internal Security and Military Power* (Ohio: Ohio University Press, 1966), p. 31.
3. Ibid., p. 35.
4. Testimony of Assistant Secretary of State Meyer, U.S., Congress, Senate, Committee on Foreign Relations, Subcommittee on Western Hemisphere Affairs, *United States Military Policies and Programs in Latin America*, 91st Cong., 1st sess., June 24 and July 8, 1969 (Washington: U.S. Government Printing Office, 1969), pp. 58–59.
5. U.S., Congress, House, Subcommittee of the Committee on Appropriations, *Foreign Assistance and Related Agencies Appropriations for 1971, Part 1*, 91st Cong., 2nd sess. (Washington: U.S. Government Printing Office, 1970), p. 307. A succinct statement on one aspect of this policy was provided by G. Warren Nutter, Assistant Secretary of Defense for International Security Affairs, in December of the same year: "Our

ability to reduce U.S. commitments abroad, and generally to lower our profile, will depend upon the caliber of training we are able to provide to foreign military personnel." See U.S., Congress, House, Committee on Foreign Affairs, Subcommittee on National Security Policy and Scientific Development, *Military Assistance Training*, 91st Cong., 2nd sess., October 6, 7, 8, December 8 and 15, 1970 (Washington: U.S. Government Printing Office, 1970), p. 132.

6. U.S., Congress, House, *Report of the Special Study Mission to Latin America on I. Military Assistance Training and II. Development Television*, p. 21.

7. U.S., Congress, Senate, Committee on Foreign Relations, Subcommittee on Western Hemisphere Affairs, *Guatemala and the Dominican Republic: A Staff Memorandum*, December 30, 1971 (Washington: U.S. Government Printing Office, 1971), pp. 7, 11. USAID officials have, elsewhere, described one of the goals of their program in Guatemala as "strengthen[ing] the government's ability to contain the security threat posed by a serious Communist insurgency movement." Quoted in Terri Shaw, "U.S. Assists Guatemala in 'Pacification program'," *Washington Post*, April 5, 1971, p. A17.

8. U.S., Congress, House, Subcommittee of the Committee on Appropriations, *Foreign Assistance and Related Agencies Appropriations for 1973, Part 1*, p. 749.

9. U.S., Congress, *Military Assistance Training*, p. 145.

   During secret hearings before the House Appropriations Committee in March 1971, Secretary of Defense Melvin Laird stated: "I think it is important for us to bear in mind that the military is the only cohesive group in many of the countries in Latin America and that they are very important." Quoted in Juan J. Walte, "Laird Cites Stability of Latin Juntas," *Washington Post*, September 7, 1971, pp. A1, A12.

10. U.S., Congress, House, Committee on Foreign Affairs, Subcommittee on Inter-American Affairs, *Cuba and the Caribbean*, 91st Cong., 2nd sess., July 8, 9, 10, 13, 20, 27, 31 and

August 3, 1970 (Washington: U.S. Government Printing Office, 1970), pp. 91–92.

11. Ibid., pp. 98–99.

12. Tad Szulc, "U.S. Navy's Visa Requests Worry Chile," *New York Times*, September 5, 1970, p. 3.

13. U.S., Congress, House, Committee on Foreign Affairs, *Foreign Assistance Act of 1971, Part 2*, 92nd Cong., 1st sess., May 11, 12, 18, 20, 1971 (Washington: U.S. Government Printing Office, 1971), pp. 420–421. According to a military attaché of one Western country, " 'when the Nixon Government realized that it could not make Popular Unity see reason, it adopted an attitude which one might objectively describe as neutral hostility, but this didn't stop Washington keeping up, and even striving to improve, its relation with the Army.' For this purpose, the U.S. gave Chile privileged treatment and posted three military attachés and half a dozen assistants in Santiago. In all, there were about thirty officers in the whole country who kept in close contact with the Navy and the Air Force, the Fach." Philippe Labreveux, "Behind the Facade of Unity," *Manchester Guardian Weekly* (Le Monde supplement), January 12, 1974, p. 15.

14. Tad Szulc, "U.S. Gives Chile Credits for Military Purchases," *New York Times*, June 30, 1971, pp. 1, 10.

15. U.S., Congress, House Committee on Foreign Affairs, *Foreign Assistance Act of 1972, Part 1*, 93rd Cong., 2nd sess., March 14, 15, 20, 21, 22 and 23, 1972 (Washington: U.S. Government Printing Office, 1972), p. 39.

16. Tad Szulc, "U.S. Is Continuing Aid to the Chilean Armed Forces," *New York Times*, December 12, 1972, p. 12. Also see U.S., Congress, Senate, Committee on Foreign Relations, *Foreign Military Sales and Assistance Act*, 93rd Cong., 1st sess., May 2, 3, 4 and 8, 1973 (Washington: U.S. Government Printing Office, 1973), p. 98.

17. U.S., Congress, House, Subcommittee of the Committee on Appropriations, *Foreign Assistance and Related Agencies Appropriations for 1974, Part 1*, p. 1198.

18. Testimony of John H. Crimmins, Deputy Assistant Secretary

of State for Inter-American Affairs. See U.S., Congress, House, Committee on Foreign Affairs, Subcommittee on Inter-American Affairs, *Aircraft Sales in Latin America*, 91st Cong., 1st sess., April 29 and 30, 1970 (Washington: U.S. Government Printing Office, 1970), p. 3.

19. See Presidential Determination No. 73-14, dated May 21, 1973, in *Department of State Bulletin*, July 16, 1973, p. 90. In commenting on this decision to sell fighter aircraft to Argentina, Brazil, Chile, Colombia, and Venezuela, Secretary of State Rogers (June 5) emphasized the necessity of lifting legislative restrictions on military sales and grants to Latin America:

> . . . we must also raise the ceiling which current legislation imposes upon military sales and grants. This ceiling is offensive to the Latin Americans who consider it an attempt to control their sovereign right to determine their own defense requirements. The only result of the ceiling has been to encourage the Latin Americans to make their purchases outside the United States.

U.S., Congress, House, Committee on Foreign Affairs, *Mutual Development Cooperation Act of 1973*, 93rd Cong., 1st sess., May 15, 17, 23, 24, 31, June 5, 6, 11, 12 and 13, 1973 (Washington: U.S. Government Printing Office, 1973), p. 257.

20. Quoted in "Suicide of Dr. Allende Reported as Army Attacks Palace and Claims Control of Chile," *London Times*, September 12, 1973, p. 1.

The junta's subsequent justification for the coup on the grounds that it prevented an imminent coup from the Left has found considerable support within the U.S. Department of Defense.

> The Allende government has been accused of playing footsie with the Cubans and the Cubans of having men in the country, and they have certainly displayed arms that they say come from Cuba, and they are reportedly still finding them, and the idea was that Allende and his

backers were going to overthrow the military in Chile so they would have complete control.

Interview No. 3–5; U.S. Department of Defense, June 10, 1974.

21. See "Chile: The Allende Years, The Coup, Under the Junta— Documents and Analysis," *IDOC* [International Documentation], no. 58, December 1973, p. 32.

22. Dan Morgan, "Junta Informed U.S. of Its Plan Before the Coup," *Washington Post*, September 13, 1973, pp. A1, A12.

23. Dan Morgan, "Coup Report Discounted, U.S. Claims," *Washington Post*, September 14, 1973, pp. A1, A13. Senator Kennedy criticized the belated and cryptic official response, pointing out that Allende "worked within the democratic system to try to effect programs to carry out [his] philosophy." Office of Senator Edward M. Kennedy, "Statement on Senate Floor Regarding Events in Chile," September 13, 1973.

24. *Department of State Bulletin*, October 8, 1973, p. 465.

25. Quoted in Terri Shaw, "Pre-Coup Activity Is Denied by U.S.," *Washington Post*, September 21, 1973, p. A26.

26. David Binder, "Allende Out, Reported Suicide; Marxist Regime in, Chile Falls in Armed Forces' Violent Coup: U.S. Not Surprised," *New York Times*, September 12, 1973, pp. 1, 17.

27. U.S., Congress, Senate, Committee on the Judiciary, Subcommittee to Investigate Problems Connected with Refugees and Escapees, *Refugee and Humanitarian Problems in Chile*, 93rd Cong., 1st sess., September 28, 1973 (Washington: U.S. Government Printing Office, 1973), p. 45.

28. Interview No. 3–6.

29. Quoted from *Congressional Record*, Senate, February 5, 1974, p. S1237.

30. Quoted in Marvine Howe, "2 Americans Slain in Chile; The Unanswered Questions," *New York Times*, November 19, 1973, p. 20. An interesting sidelight to the question of U.S.-Chilean military interaction was the following fact: "Over 100 sailors from Chile were on Guam when the Allende Government was overthrown by the rightist military in September. They were there to take charge of two former U.S. Navy LST amphibious ships. The ships formerly served in Vietnam." *Friends of Micronesia Newsletter*, Winter, 1974, p. 25.

31. U.S., Congress, Senate, *Nomination of Henry A. Kissinger,* Part 2, p. 303.

32. Szulc, "The View from Langley," p. C5.

33. Seymour M. Hersh, "CIA Chief Tells House of $8-Million Campaign Against Allende in '70–73," *New York Times,* September 8, 1974, pp. 1, 26.

34. Ibid.

35. Quoted in ibid., p. 26; our emphasis.

36. U.S., Congress, Senate, *Multinational Corporations and United States Foreign Policy, Part 1,* p. 402.

37. Ibid., p. 281.

38. U.S., Congress, Senate, *Refugee and Humanitarian Problems in Chile,* p. 39.

39. Szulc, "The View from Langley," p. C5.

40. Hersh, "CIA Chief Tells House of $8-Million Campaign Against Allende in '70–73," p. 26.

41. Interview No. 3–14, U.S. Congress, Washington, D.C., June 14, 1974.

42. Interview No. 3–16, World Bank, Washington, D.C., June 17, 1974.

43. Interview No. 3–6.

44. Interview No. 3–11, U.S. Department of State, Washington, D.C., June 13, 1974.

45. Interview No. 3–13, U.S. Department of State, Washington, D.C., June 14, 1974.

46. Interview No. 3–3.

47. Interview No. 3–14.

48. Quoted from Joseph Collins, "The Highly Visible 'Invisible' Low Profile: The Nixon-Kissinger Strategy Against Allende's Chile" (Unpublished paper, Institute for Policy Studies, Washington, D.C., February 1974), p. 1.

49. Interview No. 3–5.

50. Harry Schlaudeman, Deputy Assistant Secretary of State for Inter-American Affairs, before the House Subcommittee on Inter-American Affairs and International Organizations and Movements, June 12, 1974, in *Congressional Record—House,* June 20, 1974, p. E4051.

51. Interview No. 3–3. The U.S. government has continued to

minimize the widespread torture and other repressive policies
of the military junta, and has only reluctantly admitted that
thousands of people were killed during the coup. See "Thousands Died During the Coup in Chile, Senator Kennedy Says,"
Washington Post, February 4, 1974, p. A3. For details of the
torture, etc., and its ongoing nature, see U.S., Congress, Senate,
Refugee and Humanitarian Problems in Chile; Extracts from
the report of Amnesty International on the human rights
situation in Chile, as read into the *Congressional Record—
Senate*, January 24, 1974, pp. S423–429; Testimony of Ralph A.
Dungan and John Plank, members of an official study mission
to Chile for the Senate Subcommittee on Refugees, during
hearings before the Subcommittee on Humanitarian Problems
in Chile, as read into the *Congressional Record—Senate*, July
23, 1974, pp. S13244–13246; Laurence Stern, "Torture Reported Continuing in Chile," *Washington Post*, July 24, 1974,
p. A28; Joseph Novitski, "OAS Group Urges Chile Stop
Torture," *Washington Post*, August 4, 1974, p. A13. Also see
U.S., Congress, House, Committee on Foreign Affairs, Subcommittee on International Organizations and Movements,
International Protection of Human Rights, 93rd Cong., 1st
sess., August 1, September 13, 19, 20, 27, October 3, 4, 10, 11,
16, 18, 24, 25, November 1, and December 7, 1973 (Washington: U.S. Government Printing Office, 1974), passim; Extracts
from a new report by Amnesty International, dated September
11, 1974, as quoted in Kathleen Teltsch, "Torture in Chile
Said to Continue," *New York Times*, September 11, 1974, p.
14: extracts from a report by the International Commission of
Jurists, as quoted in "Chile Is Accused by Jurist Group," *New
York Times*, October 24, 1974, p. 11. During the 1974 foreign
assistance appropriations for Chile, there was some congressional pressure to prevent any of the disbursements from being
used for military purposes. A House amendment read, "and
none of these monies shall be used to finance military credit
sales to Chile." It was decisively defeated by a vote of 304 to
102. A Senate amendment stated that "None of the funds
made available under this Act for 'Military Assistance,' 'Secu-

rity Supporting Assistance,' and 'Foreign Military Credit Sales,' may be used to provide assistance to Chile." This amendment was agreed to. See *Congressional Record—House,* December 11, 1973, pp. H11121–H11125; *Congressional Record—Senate,* December 17, 1973, pp. S23133–S23135.

Senator Kennedy and Representative Michael Harrington are leading a campaign within Congress to eliminate all military aid to the junta during fiscal year 1975, in response to the Nixon administration's $21.3 million proposed military package to junta. See *Congressional Record—Senate,* pp. 13244–13245.

52. Interview No. 3–14. Also, Interview No. 3–12, U.S. Congress, Washington, D.C., June 13, 1974.

53. Interview No. 3–3.

54. See Jonathan Kandell, "Private U.S. Loans in Chile Up Sharply," *New York Times,* November 12, 1973, pp. 53, 55; "A Future for Business in Chile," *Business Week,* September 29, 1973, pp. 30–31; "Chile: An Uphill Struggle to Revive Business," *Business Week,* November 17, 1973, p. 41; "Chile's Offer to Return Firms Meets Favorable Reaction," *Business Latin America,* November 14, 1973, pp. 363–364. The military junta has already made an initial payment of $1.6 million to OPIC to cover compensation payments made by OPIC to other U.S. investors whose assets were expropriated by the Allende government. See "Chile: New Debts, Old Debts," *Latin America Economic Report,* March 15, 1974, p. 42. This was followed by a $321 million compensation payment to Anaconda and Kennecott. See Embassy of Chile, *Chile Today,* November 8, 1974, p. 2.

55. Interview No. 3–9, U.S. Department of State, Washington, D.C., June 12, 1974.

56. Jeremiah O'Leary, "United States, Chile Move to Forge New Links," *Washington Star,* September 25, 1973.

57. "Foreign Banks Come to Chile's Rescue," *Business Latin America,* December 12, 1973, p. 400; Terri Shaw, "Chile Gets U.S. Loan for Wheat," *Washington Post,* October 6, 1973, p. 1.

58. Richard Lawrence, "Steps Taken to Resume Aid to Chile," *Journal of Commerce*, October 17, 1973, p. 1.

59. Quoted in Shaw, "Chile Gets U.S. Loan for Wheat," p. A11.

60. Quoted in Marlisle Simons, "Chile Flour Shortage Is Grave," *Washington Post*, September 8, 1973, p. A12. Also see Marcel Niedergang, "Chile's Generals Lower the Curtain," *Manchester Guardian Weekly* (Le Monde supplement), November 10, 1973, p. 14. U.S. policy-makers were aware "that of all the imports [Chile needs] the food imports are the most critical from a political point of view in the [Allende] Government." Testimony of John H. Crimmins, Assistant Secretary of State for Inter-American Affairs, before the House Subcommittee on Inter-American Affairs, March 6, 1973. See U.S., Congress, House *United States-Chilean Relations*, p. 24.

61. Terri Shaw, "Chileans, U.S. Agree on Debts," *Washington Post*, December 22, 1973, p. A3.

62. "Chile's Foreign Creditors Okay Debt Renegotiation," *Business Latin America*, April 10, 1974, p. 115.

63. Interview No. 3–3.

64. George F. W. Telfer, "Exim Weighs Chile Action," *Journal of Commerce*, January 10, 1974, pp. 1, 3.

65. "Foreign Banks Come to Chile's Rescue," p. 400.

66. Terri Shaw, "Blockade of Chile Diminishing," *Washington Post*, October 28, 1973, pp. A1, A17.

67. Kandell, pp. 53, 55; "Foreign Banks Come to Chile's Rescue," p. 400; Everett G. Martin, "Chile's Rulers Face Huge Economic Woes, Make Some Progress," *Wall Street Journal*. A number of European countries, Canada, and Brazil also offered lines of credit to the junta.

68. "Foreign Banks Come to Chile's Rescue," p. 400. Cano quoted in "Chile Claims Favor of West's Bankers," *Washington Post*, October 8, 1973, p. A32. In commenting on the possibility of international lines of credit opening up to the junta, Assistant Secretary of State Kubisch stated:

> If the new government adopts sensible programs that can be supported from abroad, I would expect the World Bank, the Inter-American Development Bank, other gov-

ernment and international agencies, to try and assist if
that assistance is warranted.

See U.S., Congress, Senate, *Refugee and Humanitarian Problems in Chile*, p. 36.

69. Lawrence, p. 1; "Foreign Banks Come to Chile's Rescue," p. 400; "Chile: New Debts, Old Debts," p. 41; Embassy of Chile, *Chile: Summary of Recent Events*, February-March 1974, p. 8; *OAS Weekly Newsletter*, March 4, 1974, p. 3.

70. See "Chile: New Debts, Old Debts," p. 41. The junta also benefited from an extraordinary rise in the international price of copper, which reached $1.0327 a pound in November 1973. See Economist Intelligence Unit, *Quarterly Economic Review of Chile*, no. 1, March 1973, p. 9.

71. Ibid.; *Congressional Record—House*, August 6, 1974, p. H7756.

72. See "Chile: New Debts, Old Debts," p. 41.

73. Joseph Novitski, "West's Credit Flow to Chile Reopened," *Washington Post*, June 2, 1974, p. N1.

74. George F.W. Telfer, "Chile Begins Payment of International Debts," *Journal of Commerce*, July 26, 1974, pp. 1, 17.

75. "Chile's Foreign Creditors Okay Debt Renegotiation," p. 115; "Chilean Debt Renegotiated," *Latin America Economic Report*, May 10, 1974, p. 72.

76. Quoted in ibid.

77. "Enami Expansion Loans," *Latin America Economic Report*, May 3, 1974, p. 68.

78. "Chile's Foreign Creditors Okay Debt Renegotiation," p. 115.

79. *IDB News*, May 1974, p. 7.

80. Interview No. 3–9.

81. Quoted in "Latin America: loans for the good guys," *Latin America*, April 5, 1974, p. 105.

82. Interview No. 3–8.

83. Ibid.

84. Interview No. 3–11.

85. Interview No. 3–10. Also, Interview No. 3–16. ("Earlier this year, it was the case that the U.S. wanted the Bank to do more—when one didn't have the basis to judge actual performance.")

86. Interview No. 3–2. This particular World Bank official compared the abilities of the Chilean generals in the economic field rather unfavorably with those of their counterparts in Peru.

> The generals in Chile are essentially more capitalist/free market oriented and paranoid about subversion and communism, whereas the Peruvians military are much more broad-based. The Peruvian generals are trying to do a lot of things that Allende was trying to do. Also, the Peruvian generals are halfway literate. The Chilean generals are literally stupid.

87. Interview No. 3–16.
88. Interview No. 3–9.
89. Interview No. 3–8.
90. Ibid.
91. Ibid.
92. "Chile's Backing by IMF Will Help in Securing Credits," *Business Latin America*, February 13, 1974, p. 53.
93. Economist Intelligence Unit, *Quarterly Economic Review of Chile*, no. 1, March 1974, p. 20.
94. "Industrial Recession in Chile," *Latin America Economic Report*, March 15, 1974, p. 43.
95. Ibid.
96. OAS, Inter-American Economic and Social Council, Inter-American Committee on the Alliance for Progress, *Domestic Efforts and The Needs for External Financing for the Development of Chile*, CIAP Subcommittee on Chile, January 30-February 5, 1974 (Washington, D.C., OEA/Ser. H/XIV, CIAP/650, January 28, 1974), p. 91.
97. Interview No. 3–8.
98. "International Firms Cautiously Ponder Chilean Return," *Business International*, November 23, 1973, p. 371.
99. "Operation handback gets going in Chile," *Latin America Economic Report*, January 25, 1974, pp. 14-15; "Military Rulers in Santiago Are Selling 107 Companies," *The Miami Herald*, June 15, 1974, p. A17.
100. Telfer, "Chile Begins Payment of International Debts," p. 1;

Embassy of Chile, *Chile Today*, November 8, 1974, p. 2. All the major U.S.-owned plants expropriated by the Allende government, with the exceptions of the copper mines and the Ford Motor Company's assembly plant at Casablanca, have now been returned to their former owners. See "Chile: A Wobbly Economy Needs Foreign Help," *Business Week*, August 3, 1974, p. 30.

101. "Chile: New Cabinet," *Latin America*, July 19, 1974, p. 218. Also see "Chile investment law no attraction," *Latin America Economic Report*, August 9, 1974, pp. 122–123.

102. For an analysis of the attempt to restore capitalism to Chile during the first six months of military rule, based on infusions of capital and the "disciplining" of labor, see Morris Morley and Betty Petras, "Chile: Terror for Capital's Sake," *New Politics*, Winter 1974, pp. 36–50.

103. Interview No. 3–3.

7. Conclusion

1. Bernard Gwertzman, "Kissinger Calls on Latins to Join in a 'New Dialogue'," *New York Times*, October 6, 1973, pp. 1, 2.

2. In July 1974, the president of the Christian Democratic Party, Patricio Aylwin, accused the junta of treating the Christian Democrats with "systematic distrust" and complained that "our patriotic efforts to tell the government what we believe to be true and good for Chile have received no other response than repeated signs of hostility." Quoted in "Chilean Junta Challenged by Moderate Party Leader," *Washington Post*, July 18, 1974, p. A4.

3. See, for example, Joseph Novitski, "Chile Junta Deals Democracy Out of Long-Term Plans," *Washington Post*, August 2, 1974, p. A20.

4. Chile has already received proposals from U.S., Canadian, West German, and Japanese mining companies that want to invest a total of approximately $1 billion "to open new copper mines in the country . . . ." See "Chile Gets Proposals By Foreign Firms To Invest $1 Billion," *Wall Street Journal*, September 10, 1974, p. 7.